Charles Dickens (1812–70) was an author, journalist, editor and social critic, one of the most famous figures of the Victorian age. His early years were marked by poverty; aged twelve, he began work in a London blacking factory after his family were sent to debtors' prison. His first literary 'sketches', written under the pen name 'Boz', were collected and published together in 1836. Between 1836 and his death at the age of fifty-eight, he wrote fifteen hugely popular novels, including *Oliver Twist* (1838), *David Copperfield* (1850), *Bleak House* (1853), *A Tale of Two Cities* (1859) and *Great Expectations* (1861). *Our Mutual Friend* was his last completed book, published in 1865. He died at his home in Kent, and is buried in Westminster Abbey.

Ben Power is a writer and dramaturg and an Associate of the National Theatre. His plays include his Tony Award-winning adaptation of *The Lehman Trilogy* (National Theatre, West End, Broadway), D. H. Lawrence's *Husbands and Sons*, Euripides' *Medea*, Ibsen's *Emperor and Galilean* (National Theatre), *A Tender Thing* (RSC), *Six Characters in Search of an Author* with Rupert Goold (West End, International Tour), *Faustus* with Rupert Goold and *Paradise Lost* (Headlong). His screenplays include *Munich: The Edge of War* (Netflix) and the BAFTA-winning *The Hollow Crown* (BBC). From 2006–2010 he was Associate Director of Headlong and between 2014–2020 he was Deputy Artistic Director of the National Theatre.

PJ Harvey is a multi-instrumentalist, singer-songwriter, and poet. She has released ten studio albums: *Dry*, *Rid of Me*, *To*

Bring You My Love, *Is This Desire?*, *Stories From the City, Stories from the Sea*, *Uh Huh Her*, *White Chalk*, *Let England Shake*, *The Hope Six Demolition Project* and *I Inside the Old Year Dying*. Her work in theatre includes compositions for *Hedda Gabler* on Broadway; *Hamlet* and *The Nest* at the Young Vic; *Electra* at the Old Vic; *The Goat, or Who is Sylvia?* and *All About Eve* in the West End. Music for TV and film includes *Bad Sisters*, *The Virtues*, *Peaky Blinders*, and *Dark River*. In 2013, PJ Harvey was awarded an MBE for services to music. The following year, she was awarded an Honorary Degree in Music by Goldsmiths, University of London. She has been nominated for eight Grammy Awards, eight BRIT Awards, and is the only artist in history to have won the Mercury Music Prize twice. She has authored two books of poetry, *The Hollow of the Hand* and *Orlam*.

BEN POWER

London Tide

based on
OUR MUTUAL FRIEND
by Charles Dickens

songs by
PJ Harvey and Ben Power

faber

First published in 2024
by Faber and Faber Limited
The Bindery, 51 Hatton Garden,
London, EC1N 8HN

Typeset by Brighton Gray
Printed and bound in the UK by CPI Group (Ltd), Croydon CR0 4YY

All rights reserved
© Magalloway Ltd 2024
Lyrics © Polly Jean Harvey/Hot Head Music Ltd. (PRS)
and Magalloway Ltd 2024

Ben Power is hereby identified as author of this work in accordance
with Section 77 of the Copyright, Designs and Patents Act 1988

'London, My Beautiful' © F.S. Flint 1915 by kind permission of
Linda Gaisford Flint and Oliver Peers Flint on behalf of the Frank Flint Estate

All rights whatsoever in this work, amateur or professional,
are strictly reserved

Applications for permission for any use whatsoever including
performance rights must be made in advance, prior to any such proposed use,
to United Agents, 12–26 Lexington Street, London W1F 0LE

No performance may be given unless a licence
has first been obtained

This book is sold subject to the condition that it shall not,
by way of trade or otherwise, be lent, resold, hired out
or otherwise circulated without the publisher's prior consent
in any form of binding or cover other than that in which
it is published and without a similar condition including
this condition being imposed on the subsequent purchaser

A CIP record for this book
is available from the British Library

ISBN 978-0-571-39272-8

Printed and bound in the UK on FSC® certified paper in line with our continuing
commitment to ethical business practices, sustainability and the environment.
For further information see faber.co.uk/environmental-policy

2 4 6 8 10 9 7 5 3 1

London Tide was first performed in the Lyttelton auditorium of the National Theatre, London, on 17 April 2024. The cast, in alphabetical order, was as follows:

Lavinia Wilfer Beth Alsbury
Roger Riderhood Joe Armstrong
Miss Potterson Crystal Condie
Nancy Laura Cubitt
Mr Cleaver Jonathan Dryden Taylor
Charley Hexam Brandon Grace
Ensemble Miya James
Bradley Headstone Scott Karim
Reg Wilfer Stephen Kennedy
Inspector Bucket Joshua Lacey
Mary Wilfer Penny Layden
Bella Wilfer Bella Maclean
John Rokesmith Tom Mothersdale
Ensemble Liam Prince-Donnelly
Jenny Wren Ellie-May Sheridan
Lizzie Hexam Ami Tredrea
Eugene Wrayburn Jamael Westman
Noddy Boffin Peter Wight
Gaffer Hexam Jake Wood
Mortimer Lightwood Rufus Wright

Understudies
Lavinia Wilfer Ellie-May Sheridan
Roger Riderhood/Gaffer Hexam/Inspector Bucket
    Jonathan Dryden Taylor
Miss Potterson/Bella Wilfer Georgia Silver
Nancy/Movement Swing Hayley Chilvers

Charley Hexam Eric Mok
Bradley Headstone Joshua Lacey
Reg Wilfer/Noddy Boffin/Mortimer Lightwood/Mr Cleaver
   John Vernon
Mary Wilfer Laura Cubitt
John Rokesmith/Eugene Wrayburn Liam Prince-Donnelly
Jenny Wren Beth Alsbury
Lizzie Hexam Miya James

Musicians
Piano and Guitars Ian Ross
Drum Kit Alex Lupo
Keyboards Sarah Anderson

Director Ian Rickson
Set and Costume Designer Bunny Christie
Lighting Designer Jack Knowles
Composer PJ Harvey
Music Director Ian Ross
Vocal Arrangements PJ Harvey and Ian Ross
Co-Sound Designers Tingying Dong and Christopher Shutt
Movement Director Anna Morrissey
Video Designer Hayley Egan
Fight Director Terry King
Casting Bryony Jarvis-Taylor
Voice and Dialect Coach Simon Money
Associate Set Designer Verity Sadler
Deputy Music Director Jon Gingell
Staff Director Yasmin Hafesji

Characters

LIMEHOUSE

Gaffer Hexam
a Thames boatman

Lizzie Hexam
his daughter

Charley Hexam
his younger son

Miss Potterson
a publican

Roger Riderhood
a Thames boatman

Inspector Bucket
a policeman

John Rokesmith
a stranger

CHANCERY

Eugene Wrayburn
a lawyer

Mortimer Lightwood
a lawyer

HOLLOWAY

Reg Wilfer
a bank clerk

Mary Wilfer
his wife

Bella Wilfer
his eldest daughter

Lavinia Wilfer
his younger daughter

Noddy Boffin
a former servant, suddenly wealthy

BARNES

Bradley Headstone
a schoolmaster

LAMBETH

Jenny Wren
a doll's dressmaker

Mr Cleaver
her father

WINTERBROOK, OXFORDSHIRE

Nancy
a publican

LONDON TIDE

Chapter One

A SHAPE IN THE WATER

Song: 'London Song'

Company

> This is a story about money
> and of love.
> About the lies that are told
> and the truths that are hidden.
>
> This is the story of a city;
> rolling fog and moonlight.
> It's the story of souls who find themselves
> and the ones that are lost.
>
> This is a story about London,
> and of death and resurrection.
> It's a story about London –
> her stone-hard heart.
>
> This is the story of a river
> that springs from the mudbanks,
> that emerges from the marshland,
> and the secrets that lie under water
> 'neath the soft, black rain.
>
> This is a story about London,
> and of death and resurrection.
> It's a story about London –
> her stone-hard heart.
>
> It begins like this,
> with the dusk and the storm
> and the Thames . . .

The music continues. Lizzie talks to us.

Lizzie In these times of ours
(though concerning the exact year,
there is no need to be precise)
in this great hungry city
there was, one night, a storm.
The river was empty
'cept for a single filthy boat
which jerked and rolled
beneath the iron mass of Southwark Bridge.

Gaffer Keep her out, Lizzie! Tide runs strong here.

Gaffer appears in a boat.

Lizzie His eyes are fixed on the oily surface
always searching.
He hates to go home without a catch.
My job is to keep the boat straight.
Try to keep the look of dread from my face.

Gaffer Hold her steady.

Lizzie The shadows deepen as we pass London Bridge.
There's a tender yellow moonlight on the river
and suddenly . . .

Gaffer There!

Lizzie . . . it catches something,
something black and heavy in the water.

Gaffer Lizzie!

We see something floating. Lizzie climbs into the boat.

There now. Get in close.
 Closer.

Gaffer leans out and pulls the heavy object towards them. He gets a rope and begins to lash it to their boat.

Oh, but it's a fine one.
 Steady.

Not been in long, but look! Lizzie!
He didn't go in with empty pockets.

Gaffer lifts a handful of shiny wet coins up to the moonlight.

Hold this while I lash him up.
Keep your eye on it.

Lizzie I can't look at it.

Gaffer Sometimes I think you hate the river.

Lizzie No, Father.

Gaffer This water's given us everything we have in the world.

Lizzie I know.

Gaffer And again tonight it yields its treasure.

He throws something small into the water, an offering back to the river.

Now home, pull home, Liz.

Lizzie steps away from the boat as it moves off.

Lizzie I row, never looking at what we tow behind us.
I keep my head down,
as I always do on nights like this
when the rain lashes and the corpses float
and the river seems to mean only death.

Gaffer Lizzie! Pull home!

Company

This is a story about London
and of death and resurrection.
It's a story about London –
her stone-hard heart.

The river disappears.

Two lawyers are in their shared rooms. Mortimer Lightwood is at work, Eugene Wrayburn smokes and paces.

Eugene Nights like this, London's at her worst.
A beleaguered city beneath a leaden sky.

Mortimer You're in cheery spirits.

Eugene I'm *bored*, Mortimer.

Mortimer You could do some work?

Eugene Pointless.
Endless cases tried and retried.
Nothing changes.

Mortimer You knew what the law was when we trained.

Eugene The law's a guard rail
protecting the rich and powerful of this city
from the restless horde at their gate:
the poor, the hungry, the unseen.

Mortimer Have you been drinking?

Eugene There isn't enough gin in London.
I want . . .

Mortimer What?

Eugene Change. Purpose. Something.

Suddenly, a boy of sixteen – Charley Hexam – appears.

Charley Mr Lightwood?

Mortimer Yes?

Charley Nice room.

Mortimer Can I help you?

Charley Here.

Charley hands Mortimer a piece of paper. He reads, then looks at Charley.

Mortimer Is this your hand?

Charley I can write, sir. Shocking, innit?
My father told me what to put.

Eugene moves next to Mortimer.

Eugene What is it?

Mortimer My missing client.
His body's been pulled out of the river.
(*Back to Charley.*) Your father found him?

Charley And the papers that mentioned your name.

Mortimer It's certain he's dead?

Charley As a door-nail.

Mortimer Right.

Charley Though I never knew what was so dead about a door-nail.

Mortimer Young man.

Charley Coffin-nail, maybe.
Look at these shelves!

Eugene You're interested in books?

Charley I love 'em, sir.
No one who can read ever looks at a book,
even unopened on a shelf,
like someone who cannot.
It's my sister's contriving.

Eugene Then you have a good sister.

Mortimer Where's the body now?

Charley Limehouse. There's a cab outside, as long as you'll pay for it.

He holds his hand out. Mortimer gives him some coins and turns to Eugene.

Mortimer You wanted something to happen.

Eugene Me?

Mortimer Come with me.
It'll be an adventure.

Eugene Or a disaster.
Come on then.

A cab appears and the lawyers step in. Charley climbs up behind and they set off.

Charley We leave the polished stone of the Inns of Court
and the carriage rolls us down Fleet Street
past the shuttered Cathedral.
Past the Smithfield market porters
and the walls of Newgate.
Through the emptying streets
the stone arches
and the moonlit squares of the City.
Down past the Bank and the Exchange
by the Monument and the Tower.
Down over the bridge
towards the darker side of the river.

Mortimer The drowned man's name is John Harmon.
Just last month his father died
and left him a vast inheritance.

Eugene Who was the father?

Mortimer An old rascal. Made his fortune trading in dust.

Eugene Dust?

Mortimer Coal-dust, bone-dust, rough dust and sifted dust.
All the trash of London passed through his hands
and he turned it into money.

Eugene Hell of a way to make a fortune.

Mortimer He was the Golden Dustman
but an absolute tyrant to his family.
Aged sixteen, young John, the only son,

runs away abroad to escape him.
He's been gone fifteen years.
Three weeks ago, the Golden Dustman dies.

Eugene And you're handling the estate.

Mortimer Biggest case of my career.
He's left the whole pile to the son on one condition.
Harmon has to return to England
and marry a young woman he's never met.

Eugene Why?

Mortimer Total mystery.
She's no one special.
Bella Wilfer
daughter of a petty clerk from Holloway.
The son got on a boat ten days ago
to return home to an enormous fortune
and take this new wife.
I went to meet him at the dock this afternoon . . .

Eugene . . . and he never appeared.

Mortimer Now we know why.

Eugene What'll happen to the money if he's drowned?

Mortimer Old Harmon had a servant
named – don't laugh – Noddy Boffin.
He'll become sole beneficiary of the entire estate.
If this body *is* ours and Harmon *is* drowned,
then Boffin is about to become the richest man in London.
And Bella Wilfer widowed without a wedding.

The carriage continues across London.

Charley The wheels roll on.
By the docks, by Wapping, and by Rotherhithe
among vessels that seemed to have got ashore,
and houses that seemed to have got afloat,
on and on until we stop at a dark corner.
We're here.

The carriage stops.

In a small wooden house, Lizzie and Gaffer are waiting by a fire.

Gaffer Mortimer Lightwood?

Mortimer That's me. Mr . . . ?

Gaffer Gaffer Hexam.

Mortimer (*looking around*) The thing you found, is it here?

Gaffer It's close by.
The police have took possession and put into print already.
Here.

He hands him a yellow police notice. Mortimer reads.

Mortimer It says he had no money?

Gaffer Only papers.

Mortimer And his pockets were empty?

Gaffer Aye, but that's common.

He picks up a pile of other yellow posters, aged and mottled. He rifles through them.

Look.
His pockets was found empty.
And *her* pockets was found empty.
And so was this one's. And so was that one's.
I can't read nor I don't need to, for I know 'em well enough.
This one was the young woman in grey boots,
and her linen marked with a cross.
This the drunken old chap,
drowned in his slippers and nightcap.
This is them two young sisters
what tied themselves together with a handkecher.

Eugene You didn't find *all* these bodies, surely?

Gaffer looks at Eugene for the first time.

Gaffer And what might *your* name be?

Mortimer This is my friend, Eugene Wrayburn.

Gaffer Is it?
And what might Eugene Wrayburn have asked of me?

Eugene I asked you if you found all these yourself?

Gaffer I answer you: most of 'em.

Eugene And all of them missing their money?

Lizzie suddenly stands up.

Lizzie Excuse me.

She moves to the door. Eugene is in the way.

I said EXCUSE ME.

Eugene Careful, miss.

Lizzie looks at him, then pushes past and out of the house. Eugene watches her go.

Charley Don't mind my sister. She's raw tired.

Eugene Clearly.

Mortimer is looking through the pile of notices.

Mortimer These bodies you find,
has there been violence done to them,
before they enter the river?

Gaffer That's the question. You want to see tonight's catch?
Police station's over the way.
Mind you don't slip on the cobbles
I don't wanna have to pull another out tonight.

Mortimer glances at Eugene and they follow Gaffer and Charley out.

They walk, led by Gaffer, along the riverbank. Hiding under a jetty, Lizzie watches them.

Lizzie I hate hearing them talk about it
  the bodies and the money.
  I stand beneath a pier and watch them in the shadows
  as they come to the bright lamp of the police station.

Inspector Bucket appears. He stands in front of a body which is covered by a sheet. Gaffer, Charley and the lawyers join him.

Inspector No clue to how he came into the river
  but he's took an hell of a knock.
  (*Lifting the sheet.*) You see the face is mangled
  and the blood has pooled very nicely under the eyes.
  It's your young John Harmon alright.
  Name in the jacket and on the paperwork.
  Inquest'll be tomorrow.

A Stranger suddenly appears in the doorway.

Stranger Inspector!

Inspector Can I help you, sir?

Stranger There's a body?
  I may know him.

He holds up a copy of the yellow police notice.

Inspector What a chance.
  Mr Lightwood's here on that same business.

Stranger Lightwood?

Mortimer You know my name, sir?

Stranger I . . . no.

Inspector Are you seeking a Mr Harmon?

Stranger No.

Inspector Then I think you won't find what you fear to find.
  Come and have a look at him.

He lifts the sheet again and the Stranger moves forward. He glances at the corpse for a moment, then backs off, looking ill.

Turned you faint, sir?

Stranger It's horrible.

Inspector But have you identified?

Stranger No.

Inspector Who did you think it might have been?
Give us a description, perhaps we can help you?

Stranger It would be quite useless. Goodnight.

The Stranger turns towards the door but the Inspector quickly bars his way.

Inspector You won't object to leaving your name and address, sir?

Stranger John Rokesmith. Murray Wharf, Limehouse.

Inspector A rough district.

Stranger It's a boarding house.

Inspector You're just visiting London?

Stranger Just visiting.

The Inspector considers him.

Inspector Very well. Goodnight, sir.

The Inspector stands aside and the Stranger, from now on called John Rokesmith, stumbles off into the night.

Mortimer (*indicating the body*) What do you think, Inspector?

Inspector I think it's murder.
Which means anybody could have done it.
Burglary or pocket-picking wants apprenticeship.
Not so, murder. Any of us are up to that.

Mortimer (*spooked*) Indeed? Good evening.

At the door Eugene turns back to Charley.

Eugene I hope your sister feels better.

*Mortimer and Eugene go.
Lizzie is outside.*

Lizzie I see the stranger leave, pale as a ghost.

Rokesmith moves away into shadow.

Then the two gentlemen, sharing an umbrella
heading up towards the highway and a cab.

*Eugene and Mortimer move off and disappear as Gaffer
and Charley come out into the night.*

Charley and my father come out and I go quickly,
wanting to be home before them.
At the last corner before ours
Father turns towards a pub, the Fellowship Porters,
his second home.

*Gaffer separates from Charley as a pub appears. Inside,
the Landlady and other customers.*

Potterson Evening, Gaffer.

Gaffer (*nod*) Miss Potterson.

Potterson Raw cold tonight.

Gaffer Too true. I'll take a brandy.

*As Potterson fixes Gaffer a drink, another man approaches
him, unsteady.*

Riderhood Partner! I saw you on the water
and I know'd you was in luck again.

Gaffer They let you out, did they?

Riderhood I think you're like a vulture, partner, and sniff
'em out.

Gaffer Get away from me.

Riderhood Ain't been eating nothing as has disagreed with you,
    have you, partner?

Gaffer I am no partner of yours.

Riderhood Since when?

Gaffer Since you went down for robbing a man.

Riderhood Aw . . .

Gaffer (*loud*) A live man!

Potterson hands Gaffer his drink.

Potterson I want no trouble.

Gaffer holds up a hand of apology.

Gaffer (*snarled at Riderhood*) Leave me be.

He moves away from Riderhood, who holds his empty glass out to Potterson.

Potterson It being your first night out, you can take a drop
    but once that's done, on your way, Rogue Riderhood.
    I've got enough rats in the cellar.

Riderhood I've been dreaming of your sherry, Miss Potterson,
    all those nights in the cage.
    And I go by Roger now, not Rogue.
    Reformed, see?
    If I behave myself, you won't refuse to serve me.

Potterson Won't I?

Riderhood My luck's been bad, always bad.
    But the law says I'm a free man.

Potterson Luck or no luck, Roger or Rogue,
    in here I'm the law.
    One more sherry and off.

Riderhood shrugs and she pours.

Back at the Hexam house, Lizzie is by the fire. Charley enters.

Charley Alright, Liz.
Allergic to lawyers?

Lizzie Just to the lies, Charley.

Charley What a pair, eh?
You should have seen 'em as we came south.
(*He does an impression.*) Like the very air might ruin their nice shirts.
Like the water itself might rob them.

Lizzie They've probably never come across the river before.

Charley Well, I charged them double for the cab
so they *probably* won't do it again.

Lizzie grins.

Lizzie Haven't you school work?

Charley Not tonight.

Lizzie You are making the most of it, aren't you?

Charley I do my best.

Lizzie I know.

Charley And I'm grateful.
It's your contriving means Father don't suspect I'm at school.
I'm *grateful*, Liz.

Lizzie I wish I could make him believe
that learning was a good thing.

Charley He'd sooner believe that gold wasn't worth having
or beer not worth drinking.
Come 'ere to the fire.

She joins him by the fire.

See that glow? That's gas, that is,
  coming out of a bit of wood
  that's been under the mud
  that was under the water
  in the days of Noah's Ark.

Lizzie When I look at it flaring, it comes like pictures to me.

Charley I love your pictures. Tell us one.

Lizzie looks into the flames.

Lizzie Here are you and me, just little ones,
  when Father was at work and locked us out.
  We're sitting on the door-sill, huddled against the cold,
  till he comes and takes us home.
  When you're in bed, he dries my feet at the fire,
  and lets me sit by him while he smokes his pipe.
  He never once strikes me.

Charley Lucky you. What else?

Lizzie Sssshh!
  Here's a future one. Fortune-telling.
  Here's me, in this room, still holding to Father.
  I can't stop some of the dreadful things,
  but I try to keep my influence.

Charley What about me?

Lizzie Working your way at school.
  And you get prizes and you do well
  and you rise to be a schoolmaster, full of learning.

Charley There, I like that!

Lizzie But Father has discovered your studies and sent you out.
  It's divided you from Father. And from me.

Charley No it hasn't.

Lizzie I see it. As plain as can be.
Your way is not ours.

Charley I won't believe that, Liz.

She turns to him. Serious.

Lizzie I've done a good thing, to cut you away from this life, give you a new beginning.
It's the best thing I've done.

Charley We don't need to be apart though.

Lizzie You can't do better for yourself *and* keep with us.
You just can't.

Charley You'd be left just with him.
You'd choose to make yourself alone?

Lizzie I am alone. Nothing anyone can do about it.
Get yourself to bed, he'll be home soon.

She stands.

Charley Liz?

Lizzie Go to bed.

She leaves him by the fire.

Back in the pub, Riderhood leans over to Gaffer.

Riderhood What if I'd been caught robbing a dead man?
You wouldn't judge me then.

Gaffer What world does a dead man belong to? T'other world.
What world does money belong to? This world.
The dead need nothing. But it's a sneaking spirit robs a live man.

Riderhood You what?

Gaffer You got off with a short time, make the most of it.
But we'll work together no more.

Riderhood You won't shake me off.

Gaffer If I can't get rid of you one way, I'll try another.

Riderhood grabs him.

Riderhood You won't come for me, damn you!

Gaffer Let go of me.

Potterson shouts over:

Potterson Hey! I won't have it!

Riderhood releases him.

One or both of you needs to leave.

Gaffer I won't stay, Miss Potterson. Something rotten on the breeze tonight.

He walks to the door. Riderhood calls after him.

Riderhood I'll see you along the tide, Gaffer Hexam!

With a shrug, Gaffer leaves.

Potterson Out of here then, Riderhood. That's your one.

Riderhood You're cruel hard upon me, Miss Potterson. You'll let Gaffer back but not me?

Potterson Gaffer's never been where you've been.

Riderhood Oh, but he may have deserved it. He's suspected of far worse than ever I was.

Potterson Who suspects him?

Riderhood (*conspiratorial*) I tell you this.
 If you're out on the river every tide,
 and you want to find a man in the water,
 you'll greatly help your luck
 by knocking a man on the head beforehand
 and pitching 'im in.

Potterson You can't make accusations like that.

Riderhood I'll bring him to hook at last.

Potterson Get out, Rogue Riderhood.

Riderhood My name is Roger.

Potterson I said OUT.

Riderhood Alright! I'm leaving. The sherry's not as good as I remember.

He stalks off, leaving Potterson in the pub.

Potterson Time!

Lizzie is at the water's edge.

Lizzie Past midnight.
And the stranger who came to view the corpse
is standing a mile downriver, eyes on the water

Rokesmith The next day there will be an inquest.
A coroner will conclude that John Harmon came by his death
under suspicious circumstances,
though with no evidence or suspects.

Eugene A reward is offered
but no information is forthcoming.
So the case is left open and unresolved
like so many others.

Lizzie And yet it is not forgotten.

Rokesmith It's not forgotten by the stranger,
who, having given his address,
will leave Limehouse the next morning
and disappear into the London dawn.

Eugene It's not forgotten by Eugene Wrayburn, the lawyer,
who can't shake the image of the girl in the corner,
the firelight in her eyes.

Lizzie And it's not forgotten by the girl herself,
who carries the river inside her

and whose nights are haunted
by the shapes in the water.

Rokesmith From tonight, they're tied together by the invisible threads of the city.
Threads that bind us all.

Lizzie The rich and the poor

Eugene The high and the low

Rokesmith The living and the dead.

Song: 'Embers and Ash'

Lizzie

> The city is silent
> River rats creep
> The fire is dying
> It's too cold to sleep

Eugene

> Night is upon me
> Conjures the past
> Where is the future
> In embers and ash?

Rokesmith

> Mist under bridges
> Breath in the air
> A face made of shadows
> Eyes full of fear

All

> Stare into darkness
> Heart like a vault
> The rain on the window
> The fog and the salt
>
> The city is a sea
> With wrecks upon its shore

At once both deaf and loud
All night it howls for more

The city is a sea
With wrecks upon its shore
At once both deaf and loud
All night it howls for more

As the others fade into shadow, Bella Wilfer appears for the first time.

Bella

The city is a sea
I'm wrecked upon its shore
At once both deaf and loud
All night it longs for more

Chapter Two

THE MAN FROM SOMEWHERE

Bella stands alone in a widow's dress.

Bella Imagine the worst thing that could happen.
One moment you're a young person
looking to find your way in the world.
Ambitions. Plots. Dreams.
The next? This dress.
When you never saw a husband or a wedding day
or any of the benefits of being a wife.
A widow that was never married.
That's me.

Reg Wilfer arrives at the front door of his house. His wife Mary is polishing a brass plaque.

Reg Hello! What's this?

Mary It's a doorplate, RW.

Reg And a lovely shiny one. What's it for?

Mary What do you think?
It's announcing my School for Girls.
'Mary Wilfer School for Girls.'
So people know where to come.

Reg But, my dear.
You don't have a School for Girls.

Mary Not yet!
But when I do, I'll need a doorplate.

Reg How did you pay the man?

Mary It's credit, RW. What choice do we have?

Reg Perhaps, my dear, we could have saved the credit
for books or slates or other things your school might need.

Mary You're the master here, RW.
It is what you think, not what I think.
We're already reduced to renting out our bedroom,
or we would be
if you could find a lodger.
I'm only trying to make something of this family
more than accident and disaster
but *you* know best.
I'll send the doorplate back.

Reg Oh no, my dear.
It is a very fine doorplate.

They move inside the house. Lavinia is making adjustments to Bella's dress.

Mary I hope you brought something with you for supper.

Reg I did go past the butcher's, my dear,
all they had was tripe.

Mary All they had?!

Reg We can't very well afford the veal.

Mary It's your table, RW.
If you're happy feeding your daughters *tripe*.

A sudden shout.

Bella Hey! Clumsy!

Lavinia Do it yourself then.

Bella shoves Lavinia.

OW!

Mary rushes over.

Mary Oh poor Bella!

Lavinia Mother!

Reg Poor Lavinia, perhaps, my dear?

Mary Lavinia hasn't known the trial that Bella has known.
A trial without parallel in the world!

Bella You've no feeling for me, Pa!
You know what a glimpse of wealth I had,
now here I am in this ridiculous mourning.

Lavinia Oh, you . . .

Bella And yet you don't feel for me.

Reg My dear, I do!

Mary You ought to.

Bella Ridiculous.
Having a stranger coming across the sea to marry me,
whether he liked it or not,
left to him in a will, like a dozen silver spoons.
Yet it all would have been smoothed away by the money.
I hate being poor.
And we are degradingly poor,
offensively poor,
miserably poor.

Reg Steady on, Bella.

Bella I can't bear it.

She marches from the room. Suddenly, Rokesmith appears in the outer doorway.

Rokesmith Forgive me, the door was open
and there was no doorplate.
I'm seeking Mr Wilfer's house?

Before Reg can speak, Mary steps up.

Mary We're the Wilfers.
May we help you?

Rokesmith It's about the room. I saw an advertisement.

Mary Indeed? Come in. This is my husband.

Reg Evening, how do you . . .

Mary My daughter, Lavinia.

Rokesmith Is the room on the first floor still available?

Mary It certainly is, Mr . . . ?

Rokesmith Rokesmith.
 I'm quite satisfied with the room and the price.
 I wish to move in without delay.

Mary Very good. There's just the matter of a reference?

Beat.

Rokesmith I require no reference from you,
 perhaps, then, you'll require none from me.
 I'll pay in advance whatever you please.

Reg My word. Well, money *is* the best reference.

Mary Still, we'd like to see the usual kind.

Rokesmith I'm a stranger in London.
 I've none of the usual references available.

Mary Indeed?

Reg Come, my dear,
 it would certainly be to our convenience
 to resolve this matter speedily.

Mary You're master here, RW.
 Perhaps you'd like to offer the gentleman
 some of the silverware as a deposit?

Rokesmith There's no (need) . . .

Reg My wife is joking, Mr Rokesmith.
 She has a *comical* disposition.
 Here. I have the contract.

Reg fetches a paper and pen. Bella re-enters.

Mary This is my other daughter, Bella.

Bella Hello.

Rokesmith stares at her.

Mary Mr Rokesmith is taking the room upstairs.

Bella Your room?

Rokesmith If you have no objections, Miss Wilfer.

Bella Why should I care?

Reg hands Rokesmith the contract.

Reg Here we are.

Rokesmith signs.

Bella, will you witness?

Bella sighs, signs. Rokesmith watches her.

Rokesmith Much obliged to you, Miss Wilfer.

Bella Pardon?

Rokesmith For your trouble.

Bella If it were trouble I wouldn't have done it.

Awkward.

Reg That's . . . jolly good, then.

Rokesmith Eight sovereigns.

He puts the money on the table. Reg and Bella are transfixed by it.

Goodbye to you all.
Thank you again, Miss Wilfer.

Rokesmith goes. After a moment:

Mary Oh my God.

Lavinia We've got a murderer for a tenant!

Mary Or a robber at least!
Oh, RW.
I hope you won't come to regret your decision.

Reg My dears, he's just . . . diffident.

Lavinia He wasn't diffident with Bella.

Mary No! All his 'thank you, thank you'.

Lavinia 'Much obliged'!

Reg scoops up the coins.

Reg Well, diffident or not, he's given us eight sovereigns, and that means a grander supper than we planned. I'll catch the butcher before closing.

Reg puts on his coat and heads out. Mary and Lavinia begin to set the table. Reg turns back.

Did you think him odd, Bella?

Bella I barely noticed him.

Reg sighs in defeat, and leaves.

In the Fellowship Porters, Potterson is cleaning glasses. Lizzie enters.

Lizzie You asked to see me, Miss Potterson.

Potterson Sit down, Lizzie.
Bob Gliddery has made hot sausage and mashed swede. Can you eat a bit?

Lizzie No thank you, miss, I ate at home.

Lizzie sits. Potterson regards her for a moment.

Potterson I'm put out, Lizzie.

Lizzie I am very sorry for it.

Potterson Then why do you do it?!

Lizzie Me?

Potterson How often have I held out to you the chance
of getting clear of your father,
coming to live here and doing well?

Lizzie Very often.

Potterson For all you've listened
I might as well have been speaking to the iron funnel
of a steamship.

Lizzie No. Because the iron would not be thankful,
and I am.

Potterson Thankful?

Lizzie Very.

Potterson But you won't take the help!

Lizzie I won't leave him.

Potterson Do you know what is said of your father?

Lizzie What do you mean?

Potterson It is thought by some
that those he finds dead
your father *helps* to their death.

Lizzie You know that's not true!

Potterson That body last week,
the one they've put out the reward for.
They say he killed him.

Lizzie I was with him! He didn't.
He wouldn't.
Who talks like that?

Potterson Certain *characters*.

Lizzie Riderhood?!

Potterson Well, yes.

Lizzie You can't listen to *him*.
Father broke with him,
and now he revenges himself with lies.
The things that man himself has done . . .

Potterson But don't you see?!
You can't be suspicious of one
without being suspicious of the other.
They worked *together*.

Lizzie You don't know Father, miss.
He's not capable.

Potterson I know what it means to be suspected of such a thing.
For him and for you.
It's a stain that will fall over you all your life.
You won't find employment. Won't find a husband.
You'll end up on the street.
When there's killing in the family, it marks you.
Leave him, Lizzie.

Lizzie He needs me.

Potterson But you don't need him!

Lizzie *He's* my home.
I have to stay, I have to save him.

Potterson I can help you with money.

Lizzie No, miss.
Thank you but no.

Beat.

Potterson Well then, I've done what I can.
But Gaffer can't come in here any more.

Lizzie It's the only place I know he's safe.

Potterson It's been hard work to make this house what it is, and it is daily work to keep it so.

The city's changing all the time, growing, squeezing us all.
I can't risk it.

Lizzie Please, miss.

Potterson I forbid the house to Riderhood
and so I forbid the house to Gaffer.

Lizzie He didn't do those things.

Potterson I have to protect my house.

Lizzie stands.

Lizzie Believe me, miss, I *am* grateful.

Potterson Goodnight, you foolish girl.

Turning away from her, Lizzie steps out into the night.

Lizzie The night is black and shrill.
The frightful possibility comes to me
that my father, being innocent,
will be forever *believed* guilty.
I don't know if it's true or not.
But truth doesn't matter once a name is lost.
I stand on the river's brink,
unable to see into the vast blank misery
of a life suspected
but knowing it lies there dim before me,
stretching away to the great ocean, death.
It's time. Charley must go tonight.

She moves off.

The Wilfer family have finished dinner and are sitting by the fire.

Bella Why do you suppose, Father, old Mr Harmon made such a fool of me?

Reg Impossible to say, my dear.
I never exchanged more than a hundred words with him.

One Sunday in the park – you couldn't have been more than two –
   he came over, curious about the noise you were making.
   You were stamping your little foot,
   and screaming and laying into me with your wooden rattle.

Bella Was I such a beast to you?

Reg You were *making your presence felt*.
   The old gentleman appeared,
   just as you were striking me about the head,
   and said, 'That's a promising girl! A very promising girl!'
   On other Sundays when we walked his way,
   we saw him again, and . . . really that's all.

Bella Because I was such an awful child,
   he decided to marry me off to his son?
   Who in turn decided to *humiliate* me by dying!
   Preferring drowning in the river
   to lifting a veil and seeing my face?

Reg Try not to dwell on it, Bella.

He tries to pour more gin but the bottle is empty.

Lavinia Just think, Mama.
   By this time tomorrow, we'll have Mr Rokesmith here.

Mary And we can all expect to have our throats cut.

Reg Oh!

Lavinia Is there more gin?

Bella It's finished.

Reg Come on, my dears. Time for bed.

Bella I'll be a minute.

   Reg, Mary and Lavinia leave.
      Bella produces the bottle of gin she has secreted under her skirt and pours herself a glass.

Song: 'London, My Beautiful'

Bella

> London, my beautiful,
> it's not the sunset,
> nor the pale green sky
> shimmering through the curtain
> of the silver birch,
> it's not the hopping of the birds,
> nor the darkness
> stealing over.
>
> As the moon creeps slowly
> over the tree-tops,
> among the stars
> I think of her
> and the glowing of her passing
> over women and men.
>
> London, my beautiful,
> I will climb
> into the branches,
> into the moonlight,
> that my blood may be cooled
> by the wind.

She remains there, watching the night.

At dawn, Lizzie watches Charley sleeping. She has a large sack on her knee. Charley sits up in bed.

Charley Hello!
Why are you sitting there
like a ghost in the dead of the night?

Lizzie It's six in the morning.

Charley What's in that bundle?

Lizzie Get dressed and I'll tell you.

Charley Are you leaving?

Lizzie No.

Charley Who then? Not me.

Lizzie doesn't speak.

Liz. IS IT FOR ME?

Lizzie It's time.
You'll be much happier, and do much better,
even so soon as next month.
Even so soon as next week.

Charley How do you know?

Lizzie Leave Father to me, I'll do what I can with him.
But you must go. He'll be back soon.
You must go now.

She hands him coins. He looks at them.

Charley Don't make me.

Lizzie I must.

Charley I'll hate you for it.

Lizzie Don't say that!

Charley How can I not when you push me out?
You're a selfish jade!
There's not enough food or warmth for three
so you'd have me gone and all the more for you.

Lizzie I know you don't think that.
Go straight to the school, say we agreed upon it,
show what money you've brought and say I'll send more.
Whatever you hear about Father in the future
it won't be true. Remember that.

Charley I can't do it, Liz.

Lizzie You can. You will.

Charley I'm sorry for what I said,
 I know you're thinking of my good.
 But it won't be good without you.

Lizzie My job is to help you.
 You go and you succeed.
 There's no one better than you, Charley.
 Remember that.
 There's nothing else to say
 except be good, and get learning.

Charley I'm afraid.

Lizzie I know. That's as it should be.
 Think of your life here as if you dreamt it.
 The sun's rising. Time to wake up.
 Go!

Charley grabs his bundle and runs out of the door. Lizzie sits very still.
 Charley moves along the riverbank.

Charley The dawn comes on,
 and the blood-red sun on the eastern marshes
 burns like a distant forest fire.
 I don't look back.
 I run into the morning.

He goes.
 A moment after he leaves, we hear Gaffer approaching.

Gaffer Lizzie?

Lizzie I'm here.

He enters the house.

Dear, you must be frozen.

Gaffer Well, I ain't of a glow; that's certain.
 See how dead my hands are!

Lizzie Come and sit close to the fire.

Gaffer sits and looks around.

Gaffer Where's the boy?

Lizzie There's a drop of brandy in your tea.
Will the river freeze this year do you think?

She hands him a mug.

Gaffer Stays like this it will.

Lizzie That'll cause a terrible suffering?

Gaffer Suffering's everywhere forever, like soot in the air.
Ain't that boy up yet?

Lizzie Don't be angry. It seems that he has quite a gift of learning.

Gaffer You what?

Lizzie And knowing we've nothing to spare
and not wishing to be a burden to you,
he made up his mind to get some schooling.

Gaffer Did he? Schooling?

Lizzie Try to understand.

Gaffer It's unnatural, as if the river ain't enough.

Lizzie He went away this morning, Father,
and he cried very much at going,
and he hoped you would forgive him.

Gaffer Did he hope so?
He thinks I ain't good enough for him.

Lizzie No.

Gaffer Now I know why them men on the river held aloof from me.
They says to one another,
'Here comes the man ain't good enough for his own son.'

Gaffer springs up, begins to pace the room.

Lizzie That's not it!

Gaffer Then let him go.
Let him never come back to ask my forgiveness.
Let him never come within sight of my eyes
nor reach of my arm.
He's disowned his own father.
Then let his own father disown *him*.
Agh!

He turns over a chair.

Not good enough for him! It's UNNATURAL!

He turns over another chair in fury. Lizzie cowers.

Lizzie PLEASE, NO.

He stops and stares at her.

Gaffer What's the matter? You think I'd strike you?

She stares back at him.

Lizzie?

Lizzie Maybe they're right.

Gaffer Who?

Lizzie Those that call you a murderer.
I had to save him. I had to get him away
from the shame of being your son.

She runs out.

Gaffer Lizzie!

Gaffer is alone.

***Song:* 'The Burning Boat'**

Gaffer

One night I wandered London
down the bankside in a daze.

I saw a boat washed up ashore
its wooden hull ablaze.

The ancient timber crackled,
the air was thick with smoke.
I stepped onto the riverbank
to smell the burning oak.

Sing out on a London night,
Sing for the ones who burn.
Sing out on a London night,
Sing before the dawn.

I walked a little closer
and found my son sat there –
the flames reflected in his eyes,
the black soot in his hair.

My boy and I, we watched the boat
slowly turn to ash.
I held his trembling hand and said,
'All things like this must pass'.

Sing out on a London night,
Sing for the ones who burn.
Sing out on a London night,
Sing before the dawn.

And now my boy has gone away,
he heard a call and left.
His passing broke my heart in two
and I sit here unmet.

An old boat slowly burns.
An old man cries his tears.
An old boat slowly burns
And a child disappears.

Sing out on a London night,
Sing for the ones who burn.
Sing out on a London night,

Sing before the dawn.
Sing out on a London night,
Sing for the ones who burn.
Sing out on a London night,
Sing before the dawn.

Chapter Three

THE BOATMAN'S END

Morning. Mortimer is at work, Eugene is smoking.

Eugene Did you know that there are a hundred thousand children
 hungry in this town this morning?

Mortimer sighs.

You don't think that's important?

Mortimer It's a scandal. But we have work to finish.

Eugene Our work should be to improve the lives of those who need us.
 The destitute and forgotten.

Mortimer Why did you become a lawyer, Eugene?
 Why not a doctor or a priest?

Eugene You know my father came from nothing.
 I was the proof that he had made good.
 He had me down for law school before I was born.
 My first word was 'Objection!'

Rogue Riderhood enters. Out of place here in the Inns of Court.

Riderhood Lawyer Lightwood?

Mortimer Yes?

Riderhood Pardons, governor. Pardons.
 Nice room.

He sits.

Mortimer Can we help you?

Riderhood I can help *you*. If you want to know about *murder*.

Eugene Who are you?

Riderhood A man as gets my living by the sweat of my brow.
   I come to give information on the Harmon killing
   and claim the reward.

Mortimer What's your name?

Riderhood Now there you're a bit fast.
   Before I part with my name,
   can I trust my sweat will earn what it's due?

Mortimer If your information leads to an arrest,
   you'll be rewarded.
   Now, what's your name?

Riderhood Riderhood. Deptford Creek.
   I come to tell you that the hand of Gaffer Hexam,
   the hand that found the body,
   is the hand that done that deed.

The lawyers glance at each other.

Mortimer Do you have any evidence?

Riderhood I know it was him. I *know* him.

Mortimer You mean you *suspect* this man of the crime.
   He can't be convicted on a suspicion.

Riderhood What if he told me he'd done it?

Mortimer Did he tell you that?

Riderhood Night he picked up the body.
   He came to me and fell a-shaking, and he says,
   'I done it for his money. Don't betray me!'
   Those were the words.

Mortimer Why not come forward earlier?

Eugene That's easy. The reward has increased.

Riderhood Right!
Out comes the new reward
and I asks my own intellects:
'Am I to have this trouble on my mind forever?'
I give him up to you, and I want him took.

Beat.

Mortimer I'll telegram the Inspector
and ask him to meet us in Limehouse tonight.

Eugene I'll come. I want to see this adventure to the end.
(*To Riderhood.*) Gaffer Hexam has children.
Do they know of the crime?

Riderhood You never know what they know.
Especially her.

Eugene The daughter?

Riderhood Horrid thing.

Mortimer Enough. We'll meet you and the Inspector this evening.

Riderhood Come to the Fellowship.
Gaffer's sure to wash up in there.

Mortimer Very well. Thank you, Mr Riderhood.

Riderhood Mister! I like that, Lawyer Lightwood. Mister . . .

And he leaves, muttering to himself. Mortimer and Eugene look at each other.

Noddy Boffin is banging on the Wilfer door. Eventually, Lavinia appears.

Lavinia If it's creditors, we're not in!

Boffin Ho, child! Here's Mr Boffin.
I've been here half an hour.

Lavinia Who did you say?

Boffin Boffin.
BOFFIN.
Boff-In.
Is your mother home?

She calls inside.

Lavinia Mother! Not bailiffs. Boffin!

Mary rushes to the door and bustles him inside.

Mary Boffin?

Boffin Boffin.

Mary Oh, good morning, sir.
To what are we indebted for this honour?

Boffin To make short of it, ma'am,
perhaps you may be acquainted with my name,
as having come into a certain property.
Mr Harmon's property, ma'am. I own the dust.

Mary Indeed, and the gold.

Boffin And I dare say, ma'am, with the circumstances being as they are, ma'am,
and the unfortunate events regarding your daughter
that you are not very much inclined to take kindly to me?

Mary The calamity was no doing of yours, sir.

Boffin Nevertheless, I'm the beneficiary.
I am a plain sort of person, ma'am.
I don't pretend to anything, nor go round and round at anything,
because there's always a straight way to everything.
Six months ago I was a servant.
Now I have my shirts made for me by a man
who goes on holiday with the Prime Minister.
Things change.
Consequently, I make this call to say
that I shall be glad to have the honour

and pleasure of your daughter's acquaintance.
I want to cheer your daughter
and share with her such pleasures
as Mrs Boffin and I are a-going to take ourselves.
We want to brisk her up, and brisk her about, and give her a change.

Mary (*calling upstairs*) Bella! One moment, sir.
(*Upstairs again, loud.*) BELLA!

Bella comes downstairs.

Boffin Hullo hullo, Miss Wilfer!

Mary It's Mr Boffin, Bella.

Bella stares at him.

Bella What do you want?

Mary Mr Boffin wishes to offer you support, Bella,
and take you out and receive you at his house.
Isn't this something!

Beat.

Bella No.

Mary Bella?

Bella I said no.

Mary Don't be rude, dear.
(*Whispered, urgent.*) You must conquer this!

Boffin Yes! Do as your ma says and conquer it, my dear,
because we'll be so glad to have you.
We're going to move into a nice house,
and go everywhere and see everything.
You must see it all with us.

Bella Why would you do that?

Boffin Both you and I have been subject to fortune.
Mine good, yours ill.
But I want to share mine with you, do you see?

If you'd like to bring your sister with you
of course we shall be glad.

Lavinia *My* consent's of no consequence, I s'pose.

Boffin Eh?

Mary For God's sake, Lavvy,
have the goodness to be seen and not heard.

Lavinia I'm not a child.

Mary You ARE a child.

Boffin Oh dear.

Lavinia 'Bring your sister' indeed!

Mary Lavinia!

Boffin Well, well! I've made my proposal.
 Just as soon as Mrs Boffin and I are in a state to receive you, I shall return.
 And then I hope you'll do us the honour of visiting with us, just a visit, at the very least.

Bella I'll think upon it, sir.

Lavinia *As if* you won't go . . .

Mary HUSH!

Boffin Well, well, then.
 I'll be on my way.

Mary G'bye!
 (*Under her breath.*) Come on, Lavvy.

Mary and Lavinia head off. Boffin turns back to Bella.

Boffin By-the-by, miss, do you have a lodger?

Bella Yes.

Boffin Well, I may call him our mutual friend.
 I have recently begun to employ him as my secretary.
 Do you like him?

Bella Mr Rokesmith is very quiet.

Boffin Quiet, yes! Mysterious!
He arrived one day at my door
with the idea that he come and work for me,
help me run the dust.

Bella Your business is dust?

Boffin Everything discarded and thrown out by the city,
it all drifts back to me.
And it's hard work:
I didn't know I needed a secretary until I got one.
Now I find I quite like it!

Rokesmith appears.

Rokesmith Mr Boffin.

Boffin And he appears! Mysterious!
How are you, sir, how are you?

Rokesmith Well.

Nothing else.

Boffin Very good then!
Good day for the present, Miss Bella.
We shall meet again!

Boffin waves his goodbye and trundles off. Rokesmith looks at Bella.

Rokesmith Good morning, Miss Wilfer.

Bella Sir.

Rokesmith I'm glad to see Mr Boffin visiting with you.
I believe him to be a worthy person.

Bella He tells me that you work for him?

Rokesmith Yes, I've recently become his secretary.

Bella He said you turned up on his doorstep
and demanded employment.

Rokesmith Hardly demanded.
  But I thought it a good idea.
  He has a very large company to run.

Bella The dust?

Rokesmith Exactly.

Bella Are you experienced as a secretary?

Rokesmith Not especially.
  You, I think, must be an excellent writer of letters.

Bella How would you know that?

Rokesmith I noticed your hand as you witnessed
  my contract of lodging.
  A most excellent hand.
  (*Awkward.*) I wanted to say to you that I was sorry.

Bella For what?

Rokesmith Mr Boffin explained to me the circumstances
  surrounding your recent upheavals.

Bella Upheavals, sir?

Rokesmith It must be hard to bear.

Bella It was a great fortune.

Rokesmith Excuse me, I was not referring to the money.
  I meant that for someone so sure of their mind
  it must be hard to bear
  being subject to the instructions and injunctions of others.

  Beat.

Bella It is.

Rokesmith Good day then.

Rokesmith moves indoors, Bella stands in the doorway.

Bella I don't know what to make of this man.
  He has an air of incompleteness,

as if you only ever see him partially.
I know nothing about him
but these days
my every second thought is Rokesmith.

She remains, standing, as the stage darkens around her.

Evening. Riderhood and the lawyers arrive outside the Hexam house.

Mortimer Is he at home?

Riderhood He's out, and his boat's out.

The Inspector approaches them along the riverbank. Potterson is with him.

Inspector A pair of lawyers.
I'm surprised to see you
once more washed up in Limehouse.

Mortimer Inspector.

Inspector (*to Riderhood*) So you're accusing Gaffer?

Riderhood Correct.

Inspector You know that bearing false witness is a crime?

Riderhood I do. But I ain't.

Potterson You're a liar, Rogue Riderhood.

Riderhood This ain't your business.

Inspector Is Gaffer home?

Riderhood He's out on the river.

Inspector Then we must wait.

Eugene Let's not arrest him in front of his daughter.

Inspector It'll be done however's convenient.

Potterson She's the only one there now,
her brother's quit the house.

Eugene If he goes down, she'll be left alone?

Potterson Quite alone.

Riderhood (*sudden shout*) Gaffer's boat!

They peer into the darkness.

Wha' the hell?

Potterson What is it?

Inspector What, man?

Riderhood I see his boat but it's empty.

Potterson What's that it's pulling?

Riderhood What do you think? Another river catch.

Potterson A body?

Riderhood Gaffer in luck again, but no Gaffer . . .

Eugene I don't like this, Mortimer.

Riderhood Here! You see!

The boat has bobbed up to the dockside, a line running off it into the water.

Inspector Haul in, man!

Riderhood Take care, you'll disfigure 'im. Let me.

He leans in, pulls the rope. A second later, he slowly turns to them.

It's Gaffer. All noosed up.
The river's done him at last.

The men pull the body onto the shore. The Inspector turns to Riderhood.

Inspector Run to the station.
Tell the constable I need him here.

Riderhood Christ, it's done him at last.

Riderhood runs off.

Inspector Miss Potterson, send word to the Coroner.

Potterson (*shaken*) Yes, sir.

Potterson steps back inside. The Inspector kneels by the body.

Mortimer Did someone do this, Inspector?

Eugene It looks more like he did it to himself.

Inspector Fell overboard in one of these heavy squalls
and tangled his neck in his own slip-knot.
With every wave, the knot tightens
and his own boat tows him dead.

Mortimer An accident then?

Inspector All I know is that it's very nasty.

Suddenly, Lizzie appears on the riverbank.

Lizzie Inspector?

Inspector Oh miss. I'm afraid it's bad.

Lizzie What happened?

Mortimer I'm so sorry.

Lizzie kneels next to Gaffer.

Lizzie Dear, you're so wet and cold.
What's that? Did you speak?

She leans her ear close to the dead man's mouth and listens.

Mortimer (*to Lizzie*) Is there anyone we can fetch for you?

She doesn't respond.

Inspector We'll leave him here.
The constable will come along and take charge of him.

Mortimer Eugene, I . . .

Unable to speak, Eugene moves into the shadows.

Inspector Seems that your friend has no stomach for it.

Mortimer If you've no further need of me, Inspector, I'll say good night.
I'm sorry for your loss, Miss Hexam.

Still nothing. He goes.

Inspector The constable'll be along.

The Inspector goes too. Lizzie is alone with the body.

Song: 'Lizzie Alone'

Lizzie

Shadows rise unbidden
I watch the angels drown
And I won't sleep tonight or ever
I have forgotten how

The tide brings in the darkness
The nameless river fear
Why has the boatman left me?
Why am I still here?

Early morning terror
And then the midnight shame
Tell me, tell me, Father
How do people change?

I'll stay here in the dark now
The past is locked away
Keep behind the curtain
The future is unmade

How do people change?
How do people change?

Chapter Four

ON THE SUBJECT OF EDUCATION

Bella is in the Boffins' living room.

Bella Since my first invitation
   I've become something of a fixture
   at the house of Mr and Mrs Boffin.
   For the last three weeks I've stayed here
   and not once been home.
   We go to the park or to the theatre almost every day.
   I confess I find it most agreeable.

Boffin bustles in.

Boffin Ho ho! Miss W!
   Have you had your tea?
   Will we take it together?

Bella That would be lovely.

Boffin My morning has been bewildering.
   I seem to have become involved in local politics!

Bella How interesting.

Boffin Is it? I find politicians a queer set.
   They've chosen a life of service
   it seems only in order to serve themselves.
   I know they want my money
   but Mrs Boffin likes the parties.
   Have you seen my secretary?

Bella Not today.

Boffin He's an invaluable man, Rokesmith.
   But I can't quite make him out.

Bella What do you mean?

Boffin The other afternoon, he went very strange.
We had news come about the case.

Bella About John Harmon?

Boffin Oh my dear, yes.
I'm sorry to drop it on you like a hot cake.
But they know who did it.
The murder.

Bella I see.

Boffin Seems a docklands boatman
bashed him on the head for his purse.

Bella Is the man arrested?

Boffin No, that's the grisly thing.
They went to catch him,
found him dead in his boat.

Bella Then the whole thing is over.

Boffin For him. Of course his family'll suffer.
My lawyer Lightwood tells me that there are children.
They'll find their lives marked by their father's crime.

Bella And Mr Rokesmith . . .

Boffin Was quite turned by the news.
White as a sheet, muttering to himself.

Bella Perhaps he does not like to hear of death.
He must have led a sheltered life.

Boffin Who knows what kind of life?
He's a closed book.
Objects to speak to anybody except me and Mrs Boffin.
And you, of course. Always interested in you.
I fetch the tea!

Boffin goes.

Bella Not very long ago
   I felt fluttered by the possibility
   that my father's lodger took an interest in me.
   But that was before my new life of cafés and parks and theatres.
   Now I find his manners very intrusive.
   He's always staring . . . Oh!

Rokesmith has appeared, staring at her.

Rokesmith I had a thought, Miss Wilfer.
   As I'm back and forth between here and your family
   I'd be happy to execute any commands
   you may have in that direction.

Bella Commands?

Rokesmith Any words of remembrance?

Bella They don't send any words of remembrance to me.

Rokesmith They frequently ask me about you.
   I think your mother and sister
   are much distressed by your absence.

Bella I doubt it, sir.

Rokesmith You underestimate them.

Bella I don't think so.

Rokesmith Perhaps you ought to contact them?

Bella Ought I?!

Rokesmith It would be the kindly thing to do.

Bella Enough!
   It so happens that I am going to see them today.

Rokesmith Really?

Bella I've arranged a small lunch party.
   So you can keep your words of admonishment to yourself.
   Perhaps you would tell Mr Boffin
   I won't be needing the tea.

Rokesmith I'll tell him so.

Beat.

I'm sorry if I spoke with too much force.

He nods and leaves. Bella thinks for a moment.

Bella I'd not thought of seeing my family until he mentioned it.
Now I have to.
As if I don't want to be shamed in his eyes.
What does that mean?
Why do I mind what he thinks when I don't care for him?
He *infuriates* me.

She walks out.

Charley is standing on the riverbank with Bradley Headstone.

Charley In the warmth of a summer's morning,
two scholars cross the river at Lambeth Bridge.
We stand for a moment and watch the explosions
as they build the Great Embankment,
men trying to tame the river.
(*To Bradley.*) Thank you for coming with me,
Mr Headstone.
I want you to judge my sister for yourself.

Bradley Does she work?

Charley She wrote me that she'd found a job in a stockroom.
When my father passed,
she had to leave Limehouse . . .

Bradley Because of the allegations.
No one at school knows about that, Hexam.
Keep it that way.

Charley Yes, sir.

Bradley She's in a boarding house?

Charley A place in Lambeth.
Just temporary.

Bradley A house for fallen women?

Charley She ain't fallen, sir.
I don't know what kind of place it is.

Bradley Listen to me, Charley.
In good time you are sure to pass an examination
and become a teacher.
The school we work at, and schools like it,
are academies of order, discipline.
If you wish to thrive, you cannot afford an *unmoored* family life.
You can't give any ammunition to those that would cut you down
These things matter.

Charley Lizzie's not unmoored. She's the reason I'm here.

Bradley Your future's important to me, Hexam.
I see something of myself in you,
pulling yourself from the mire
up towards the pure light of respectability.

Charley checks a scrap of paper.

Charley This is the address she gave me, sir.

Bradley The smell's devilish.

Charley Hello? Anyone here?

In the corner of a dark room, Jenny Wren sits.

Jenny Hello hello. I'm the person of the house.
What did you want?

Charley To see my sister.

Jenny Many young men have sisters. Give me your name.

Charley Charley Hexam.

Jenny I thought it might be. Your sister's my particular friend.
Who's this gentleman?

Charley Mr Headstone, my schoolmaster.

Jenny Fancy. She'll be back. Take a seat.

She goes back to work. They watch. She grins at them.

I am full of mysteries.
I bet you can't tell me the name of my trade.

Bradley You're making something with straw.

Jenny Ah but *what* am I making?

Bradley Table mats?

Jenny Table mats!? Try again.

Bradley Ladies' bonnets?

Jenny Almost! Bonnets and dresses for the finest ladies. For dolls!

Bradley Dolls?

Jenny I'm a doll's dressmaker.

Bradley and Charley look at each other.

Bradley I hope it's a good business?

Jenny Poorly paid. And I'm so pressed for time!
I had a doll married last week,
and I was obliged to work all night.
Then the bride-doll started moaning about the fit of her dress . . .

Lizzie enters the house.

Now here's my particular friend!

Lizzie Hello, Jenny.
(*Seeing Charley.*) Charley!

She runs over and embraces him.

Charley There, there, Liz.
Look. Here's Mr Headstone come with me.

Bradley nods, awkwardly.

Jenny Don't she look well? Much less pale now . . .

Lizzie I didn't expect a visit.
I hope Charley does well, Mr Headstone?

Bradley He could not do better.

Lizzie So well done of you, Charley!

Bradley Your brother is very much occupied.
The less his attention is diverted from his work,
the better.

Lizzie I always said as much.

Charley Never mind that.
How are you getting on?

Jenny Oh, she's getting on well. Very well!

Charley You have your own room?

Lizzie Upstairs. It's very pleasant.

Charley looks sceptical.

Jenny And she always has the use of this room for visitors.
I was only saying to my dolls this afternoon:
'When will Lizzie have a visitor?'
And they said . . .

Charley Perhaps we should go out into the air, Liz?
It was nice to meet you, miss.

Jenny does a little bow. Bradley looks uncertainly at her.

Jenny So the thing about dolls . . .

Bradley I'll come with you, Hexam.

Jenny Good day, Mr Schoolmaster.

They leave the house and move out along the river.

Bradley I'll be over there. We don't have long, Hexam.

Bradley moves aside. Charley looks at Lizzie.

Charley I'm sorry about the funeral, Liz.
The school wouldn't . . .

Lizzie No one came, Charley.
Just me, Father in his box and a dozy priest.
The Inspector stood to one side, staring.
Accusing.

Charley None of his old friends?

Lizzie He's marked as a murderer.
No one would talk to me 'cept Miss Potterson.
She wanted me at the pub, but I couldn't stay.
Not so close.
So I found lodgings here.

Charley When are you going to settle yourself
into a more Christian sort of place?

Lizzie I'm very well where I am.

Charley I never thought I'd find you in such company.
Who is she?

Lizzie You remember the bills Father kept at home?
Notices of those that had drowned?

Charley What of them?

Lizzie Jenny's the grandchild of the old man.

Charley What old man?

Lizzie The terrible drunken old man
that drowned in his slippers and night-cap.

Charley What does that have to do with anything?

Lizzie Her father's weak and wretched,
   falling to pieces, never sober.
   This poor creature has been surrounded by drunks from her cradle . . .

Charley I don't see what *you* have to do with her.

Lizzie Don't you?!

Charley Not in any way!

Lizzie She loved her grandfather in spite of his infirmities.
   He drowned and we hauled him out.
   We stole the little he had.
   I have to make some form of . . . restitution.

Charley Restitution?

Lizzie We're *bound* to the river, Charley.
   Our cradle, Father's grave.
   It runs through me and . . .

Charley I can't bear it when you speak like this.
   I am trying my best to get up in the world,
   and you pull me back.

Lizzie Me?

Charley I don't want you here, Liz.
   I'm ashamed to have brought Mr Headstone with me.
   He can help you
   if you are sober and sensible and leave these fancies behind.

Lizzie There's a stain on us, Charley.
   Father's sins marked us with blood forever.
   I can't get away from it.

Charley It's a choice!
   You taught me to fight it. You sent me away.
   Now you've chosen to lodge yourself
   with people like this
   and you talk as if you were drawn here against your will.
   Give it up, Liz!

Silence.

GIVE IT UP.

Lizzie I'll try. What is it?

Charley I'm sorry, I don't mean to shout.
I know what I owe you.

Bradley returns.

Bradley Hexam?

Charley We can go now, sir.

Bradley Will you walk some of our way with us, miss?
I was hoping we might converse a little.

Lizzie I must get inside. You'll go faster without me.

Bradley Another time.

Lizzie Thank you for taking care of my brother,
Mr Headstone.
I appreciate it so very much.

Bradley He's a good student.

Lizzie And you must be a very great teacher. Goodbye,
Charley.

She disappears. They watch her go.

Charley Did you hear our words, sir?

Bradley Your sister scarcely looks or speaks like an ignorant person.
But she is clearly a dreamer.

Charley It's painful to think that I could get on as well as you hope,
and come to be embarrassed by her.

Bradley She needs tutelage.
Perhaps we might consider what I could do for her.

Charley You'd help her, sir?

Bradley Not at the school, of course.
But private lessons, perhaps.

Charley I'd be so grateful.

Bradley I know something, Hexam,
of what it is to transform yourself.
Of the sacrifice and the stoicism needed.
Indeed, I know of that.

Charley Yes, sir.

Bradley We're expected back at school.

Charley nods and leaves. Bradley looks at us.

Structure and discipline. Order and regiment.
Just as I pulled myself from the mire
so I'll shape these poor souls.
I'll shape this world with my own hands
or burn up in the attempt.

Song: **'Bradley Headstone'**

Bradley

Once there was a lonely prince
His head hung low
His back was hunched
His face was pale

He'd look away when others came
Hid in the dark
His heart on fire
Too afraid

Company

They covered him in feathers
They tarred and scarred his skin
But he never turned
To look at them
He stared straight at the sun

Bradley

> The prince he grew to adulthood
> He dried his tears
> He hid his fears
> Became a king
>
> The king became an iron rod
> With certainty
> And learning
> Held in his fist

Company

> But he never looks behind
> He's running out of time
> For one day they'll come
> And drag him home
> The ones who know the truth
>
> They'll cover him in feathers
> They'll tar and scar his skin
> But he'll never turn
> To look at them
> He'll stare straight at the sun.

Bradley follows Charley off.
Lizzie re-enters the house.

Jenny Well, Lizzie, what's the news out of doors?

Lizzie It's stopped raining. What's the news indoors?

Jenny The big news is: I don't mean to marry your brother.

Lizzie No?

Jenny No-o. Don't like the boy.

Lizzie What do you say to his schoolmaster?

Jenny He's what Jenny Wren calls
'Mighty Particular'.

Lizzie laughs. Jenny stops sewing for a moment.

Not like Mr Eugene Wrayburn, your other visitor.

Lizzie Jenny.

Jenny He's dashed in from the pages of a romance!
Jumped off his white horse and here to save us!

Lizzie He's just a lawyer.

Jenny A lawyer who keeps finding reasons to visit you.
'I bought you a book, my dear Miss Hexam,
Oh hello Miss Wren, I didn't see you there.'

Lizzie He helped me after my father's death.
When no one else in Limehouse would speak to me
he and Miss Potterson were my friends.

Jenny He wants to whisk you off!

Lizzie I've no intention of leaving, Jenny.

Jenny Don't say that.
When they say that they always go directly.

Eugene enters.

Eugene Miss Hexam. Miss Wren.

Jenny Ooh look, Lizzie. What a surprise.

Lizzie elbows her sharply.

Lizzie (*jumping in*) Is there news about my father?

Eugene Ah. No. On that, I have nothing to report.
I'm sorry.

Lizzie I thought perhaps . . . Never mind.

Eugene Did I just see your brother on the bridge?

Lizzie He was visiting with us.

Jenny With a schoolmaster.

Eugene Why did Charley bring a schoolmaster here?

Lizzie I think Mr Headstone needed to assure himself
   that, although I might not be learned,
   I'm not a completely bad influence.

Eugene The damn nerve!
   When you've been the very best of influences.

Jenny I'd like to show that schoolmaster.
   If only we could become learned, Liz . . . imagine.

Eugene Indeed *do* imagine, Miss Hexam.
   Jenny, you have hit upon the exact purpose of my visit.
   I have been, of late, *dissatisfied*,
   deeply bored, of my life in the law.
   But I have a notion.

Lizzie A notion?

Eugene I propose to be of some use to somebody in this world
   and I propose that person should be you.
   My notion is that I could come here certain nights in the week,
   and give you instruction and learning.

Jenny claps with delight.

Jenny That IS a notion!

Lizzie I don't . . .

Eugene (*quick*) I anticipate your response!
   You're going to say no.
   Because your humility prevents you accepting something good.
   You know schooling to be good
   or you'd never have devoted yourself to your brother's having it.
   So, why not have it yourself?
   Especially when Miss Jenny here could profit by it too.

Jenny Yes!

Lizzie Is it proper?

Eugene If I were to meet either of you *alone*
or with an intention other than education
it would not be proper.
As it is, it is entirely fit.

Lizzie shakes her head.

Lizzie I'm sorry.
I won't be in anyone's debt.

Eugene There's no question of debt. Just consider . . .

Lizzie No, sir. Don't ask again.

Eugene If you would only listen!

Lizzie NO, SIR.

Beat.

Eugene Very well.

He moves to the door. Stops.

I will say only this.
Don't be shamed by an ungrateful brother
who brings schoolmasters here
like doctors to look at a bad case.
Go to work and improve yourself.
For the sake of your late father.

Lizzie My father?

Eugene Don't keep the deprivation
to which he condemned you
forever on his head.

Lizzie Please don't.

Eugene I don't want to distress you.
I'm sorry.
I really did mean well.

Lizzie I don't doubt that.

Eugene Then why do you refuse?

Lizzie hesitates.

Think again.

Jenny leans towards Lizzie.

Jenny Oh, let's become learned, Lizzie.

Lizzie looks at her.

Why should only the boys be allowed to read?

Lizzie nods slowly.

Lizzie I hope you won't think the worse of me for having hesitated.
I accept.

Eugene Yes? Ha! I am happy!
Though it is only a little thing, I am happy.
We may begin next week.

A noise outside. Jenny looks up in alarm.

Jenny The issue being resolved, Mr Wrayburn,
we won't detain you.

Eugene I'm sorry?

Eugene looks at Lizzie, confused.

Lizzie (*whispered*) Her father.

Eugene Very well. I'll come next week and bring books.
I'm happy!

Eugene leaves, delighted. As he goes, he bumps into an older man entering the house.

Excuse me.

Mr Cleaver Careful!

Lizzie immediately stands.

Lizzie I'll leave you, Jenny.

Mr Cleaver Don't go, Miss Hexam, it ain't catching.
How's my Jenny?
Will you give your affection to a broken-hearted invalid?

Jenny I can smell you from here!
Ain't you ashamed of yourself?

Mr Cleaver Yes, ashamed.

Jenny Put down your money this instant.

He starts to look in his pockets. Hands her coins.

Is this all?

Mr Cleaver Got no more.

Jenny Get along with you!
I'm not going to forgive you.
Go to your bed this moment!

He crawls off.

What will I do, Lizzie,
if my husband should turn out like that?

Lizzie Oh he won't.

Jenny I tell you what I'd do.
When he was asleep, I'd make a spoon red hot,
and I'd have some boiling liquor bubbling in a saucepan,
and I'd pour it down his throat,
and it'd blister him and choke him.

Lizzie You would do no such horrible thing.

Jenny You haven't lived among it.
Still. I have you.

Lizzie You do, my dear.

Jenny Come and help me with these dresses.
The buttons are a fiddle
and the dolls will be furious if they aren't done right.

Lizzie moves over to help her.

The Wilfers are preparing a picnic.

Mary Well, look at the time.

Reg She said she'd be here.

Lavinia Do we have to wait?

Reg That would be kind, my dear.

Lavinia I'm *starving*.

Mary The food'll spoil! But you're the master here, RW. If you're happy with your daughters eating off-food . . .

Reg Here she is. Bella!

Bella enters.

Mary Well hello, Stranger.

Bella Hello, Ma. Pa. Hello, Lavvy.

Lavinia Lavinia!

Mary Quite an honour to see you. You'll find your sister grown.

Lavinia Urgh, don't talk nonsense, Ma.

Mary Hear that?
One child of mine deserts me for the proud and prosperous,
the other despises me.

Lavinia Oh don't start!

Reg Mary.

Bella Mr and Mrs Boffin may be prosperous,
but they're not proud.
Really, Ma, they are very decent.

Mary Truly we are *required* to think so.

Lavinia '*Required*'!

Reg My dears.

Mary What?

Bella Don't be cruel.

Mary Us cruel?
It's not us who's abandoned our family
in favour of the perfect Boffins.

Reg Shall we settle to eating?

Lavinia What do you *do* over there with them?

Bella We go to the theatre and to cafés.
Mrs Boffin takes me shopping . . .

Mary Oh stop, I shall faint.

Bella I'm only answering.

Mary Only breaking your mother's heart!
I wonder that you found time to tear yourself away.

Bella I won't again if this is the welcome.

Lavinia I knew it. She *hates* us!

Mary bursts into tears.

Mary Oh Lavvy!

Lavinia They've set her against us.
Detestable Boffins, disreputable Boffins, beastly Boffins.

Lavinia too burst into tears.

Mary (*between sobs*) Come on, Lavvy, get out the things.
Might be our last meal as a family . . .

Lavinia Why do I have to do it?

Mary Don't even begin!

They move away to unpack the food.

Reg Come, Bella, I'm very pleased to have you with us.

Bella And I'm pleased to see you, Pa.

Reg Have we lost you from the house for good?

Bella I don't know.
I fear I might be the most mercenary wretch
that ever lived in the world.

Reg I should hardly have thought that.

Bella I was so unhappy for so long.
Now at the Boffins I'm supplied with everything I could want.
Their charity has made me so comfortable
that I cannot think of leaving them.
I should be content.
And yet I cannot settle.

Reg You've had a tempestuous few months, my dear.
Of course the comforts of the Boffins are lovely.

Bella I don't deserve them.

Reg I say that you do.
There's time enough to think of starting out.
For now, enjoy yourself.
Only think kindly of your mother and sister.

Bella I will try.

Mary and Lavinia carry the food over.

Mary It's only pork pies.
Not what you're used to.

Reg Mary.

Bella They look delicious, Ma.

Lavinia I helped make them.

Bella Thank you.

Reg Now, that's nice.

Bella And in fact, Mr Boffin likes a pork pie.
We often have them at home.

Mary Home? Home? Oh no!

Mary bursts into tears again.

Reg Oh dear.

Lavinia Home! Oh Bella!

And Lavinia bursts into tears again.

Bella Come now!
It's not that I don't miss you all . . .
Here, I bought this.
(*Hands Reg purse.*) Buy presents for everyone.

Lavinia and Mary immediately perk up.

Lavinia What's that?

Reg Are you sure?

Bella Sure.

Reg Thank you, my dear girl.

Mary I'll take it.

Lavinia That doesn't fix it.

Bella I know.

As her family examine the purse, Bella steps out and Greenwich disappears.

We sail back into town
and I leave them on the dockside at Blackfriars.
In the pale wash of evening
as I watch them walk away
tears fill my eyes.

Reg walks away.

Poor dear struggling little Pa. And poor Ma and Lavvy.
   So entirely themselves.
   I'm caught between two worlds.
   And as I head back to the warmth of the Boffins
   I know I don't belong to either.

Bella enters the Boffin house. Rokesmith is standing in the hall.

Rokesmith Miss Wilfer.

Bella jumps.

Bella You startled me.
   Are you . . . waiting for me?

Rokesmith I'm not.

Bella Are Mr and Mrs Boffin in?

Rokesmith Gone to a reception in Holborn.
   Just me here.

Bella I expect you'll want to be getting away.

Rokesmith I'll stay for a while.
   There is a lot to resolve in Mr Boffin's inheritance.

Bella He told me they found the man who killed John Harmon.

Rokesmith They did.

Bella And he is dead?

Rokesmith That story is over.

Bella Not for his children.

Rokesmith What do you mean?

Bella They will be scarred by their father's crime.
   They will run from it their whole lives.
   It's not fair.

Rokesmith So much about this situation is unfair.

Bella I wish there was something that could be done for them.

Rokesmith Indeed.

Beat.

Bella I'm sorry if I was curt with you earlier, sir.
It was kind of you to suggest that I contact my family.

Rokesmith It was nothing.
I mean, it was my pleasure.
I think that despite an occasional surfeit of feeling your family are very estimable indeed.

Bella You do?

Rokesmith My family was not . . . warm.
You are lucky to have them.
And they you.

Bella doesn't know what to say.

Good evening, Miss Wilfer.

He goes upstairs to the study. Bella goes into the garden.

Song: 'Evening'

Bella

Six in the evening
Watching him working
Up at the window
Lit by a candle
Ink across parchment
I feel like I'm floating

Everything's formless
Shapeless and shifting
You are a stranger
You are a stranger
Your eyes on the paper
You blow out the candle

Rokesmith
>Six in the evening
>Watching her standing
>Down in the garden
>Under the beech tree
>Breeze through the branches
>I feel like I'm falling
>
>Deep under water
>Everything's heavy
>Dark, unforgiving
>Here I know no one
>But you are familiar
>You walk from the garden

Both
>I turn from you
>You turn from me.
>
>*Bella leaves. Rokesmith steps towards us.*

Rokesmith I leave the house after night has fallen,
and walk for hours
down to the river.
To Deptford Creek.

He is alone by the river.

I stand in the darkness and watch the water move
>belonging more to this place of death
>than the halls of the living.
>
>John Rokesmith is made of shadows.
>My real name is John Harmon
>and I have been five months dead.
>
>I was barely a man when I left England.
>My father was a brute,
>but in the years since I ran away,
>I'd almost forgotten the ice of his grip.

The news of his death
and my poisoned inheritance,
 the woman he was forcing me to marry,
pulled me back towards London
and his kingdom of dust.
Onboard ship, I took to opium
numbing the dread of this awful future.
As we docked, instead of meeting my fate,
I slipped away from the crowd,
The lawyer appointed to meet John Harmon
was left waiting at the water's edge.
I went looking for oblivion,
determined to escape my father forever.

I came to a doorway, a flight of stairs, a room.
The night was miserable and it rained hard.
I tasted my pipe, the sickly sweet fumes
removing all care and weight from the world.
I sat in my stupor and watched as if dreaming
as a gaunt young man rose from the corner
and crawled towards me.
He grabbed my bag, my money, my papers, my coat.
I tried to object but my body moved as if underwater.
He ran from the room.

Barely able to walk, barely able to see, I followed,
falling down the stairs, out into the night
swooning and reeling across the wet cobbles.
Through the opium blur,
I saw the thief running away and colliding into a man.
A riverman with a haunted face
and a great serpent tattooed on his arm.
Suddenly they were fighting
the serpent reached out of the darkness and struck the thief
struck him again and again.
He took money – my money –
then heaved the body into the water.
I watched the water fill his lungs

I watched the body sink.
I watched myself die.
The riverman disappeared into shadows
and I passed out on the stones.

When I came to, it was still dark.
I saw a yellow police notice nailed to the wall.
It told of a wealthy man found dead that night in the river
now lying in the mortuary.
A man named John Harmon.
As the drug fog cleared,
I saw that the river had handed me a gift.
The thief had died my death for me
and now lay bloated and grey on the tiles.
John Harmon was drowned and John Rokesmith was born.

Now there is Bella, my widow.
She talked about the dead boatman accused of murder
and his children, forever marked by his supposed sin.
I alone know he was innocent.
For her and for them, I must do something.

We see Charley, working with Bradley. Eugene, teaching Lizzie and Jenny. Bella sits up, alone, in Hampstead. They all remain onstage through the following . . .

So I return to Deptford Creek.
And I wait.

Riderhood comes walking along the riverbank. Rokesmith steps in front of him.

You.

Riderhood I don't know you.

Rokesmith No, you don't.

Riderhood If you mean to scare me
then you don't know me, neither.
I've nothing worth robbing so what do you want?

Rokesmith The truth.

Riderhood You're in the wrong part of town.

Rokesmith I know you're lying about the Harmon murder.

Riderhood Do you?

Rokesmith You falsely accused Gaffer Hexam.
You know why and I know why.
The river serpent crawling up your arm knows why.

Riderhood What do I care for what you know?

Rokesmith You'll care if I tell my story.
You'll lose your reward and worse will follow.
False witness is the least of your crimes.

Riderhood He came at me. I defended myself.

Rokesmith You killed him, picked his pockets and rolled him into the river.

Riderhood Who are you?

Rokesmith Nobody.

Riderhood Then I've nothing to say to you.
Gaffer Hexam's dead. My partner's dead!
How can my words hurt a dead man?

Rokesmith They hurt his living children.
You'll testify that what you have sworn
against their father is utterly false.

Riderhood You don't scare me, Nobody.
You're made of shadows!

Rokesmith I am. And I will fall here again.
Testify the truth about Hexam
or I will tell my story and it will destroy you.
Get into your hole.

Riderhood Gah!

With a shrug, Riderhood pulls himself away. Rokesmith turns to us.

Rokesmith My heart is pounding. I don't feel the cold.
 The waters are rising and will soon burst their banks.
 My name is John Harmon.
 Could I return to life? Could I be reborn?
 If I were, the money would be mine
 and Bella Wilfer sordidly purchased.
 She'd hate me. Or maybe not . . .
 I must find out how I stand with her.
 I swore to myself never to raise these ghosts.
 But the dead will not lie in peace.

The light fades.

Interval.

Chapter Five

AFFAIRS OF THE HEART

Eugene is alone.

Eugene I visit Lizzie Hexam two evenings a week.
 By the light of the setting sun on the river
 we read Ovid and Virgil, Shakespeare and Donne.
 She loves the stories of transformation and metamorphosis.
 I'm her teacher. She's my pupil.
 But when she reads . . . she becomes something else.
 Sometimes she catches me staring.
 I can't help it.

He rounds a corner to find Charley and Bradley waiting for him.

Charley Hexam?
 Why are you standing outside my chambers
 like a ghoul in the dark?

Charley I've something to say and I mean to say it.

Eugene And who may this other person be?

Bradley Charles Hexam's schoolmaster.
 Worthy of your respect, Wrayburn.

Eugene You know my name, what's yours?

Bradley That doesn't concern you.

Eugene True, it doesn't concern me at all.
 I'll call you Schoolmaster.

Charley I had a plan for my sister's education.
 My friend here was to be her tutor.

And when I come to arrange lessons,
what do I find?
That she is already being taught.
What are your intentions to my sister?

Eugene Intentions?

Charley I cannot have darkness cast upon my prospects.

Eugene Do I cast darkness?

Charley As I raise myself, I intend to raise her
and I don't want her to be grateful to you
or to be grateful to anybody but me and Mr Headstone.
You don't take heed of what I say, it'll be worse for her.
LEAVE. HER. ALONE.
There. I've said what I came to say.

Eugene Indeed, you've said plenty.

Bradley Go back to school, Hexam. Give me a moment with him.

Charley leaves. Bradley eyes Eugene.

You think us of no more value than the dirt under your feet.

Eugene I assure you, Schoolmaster,
I don't think of you at all.

Bradley That lad could put you to shame
in half a dozen branches of knowledge in half an hour,
but you think him your inferior.
You think the same of me, I've no doubt.

Eugene As I say, I don't think of you, Schoolmaster.

Bradley My name is Bradley Headstone!

Eugene Is it?! I know your type.
I know the violence you do when you improve people.

Bradley Do you?

Eugene You learn by rote and teach by rule.
What was it you were planning to teach Lizzie Hexam?

Bradley I'm helping to raise this family.

Eugene They are already far above you.

Mortimer appears around the corner. Sees Eugene and Bradley eyeballing each other.

Mortimer Eugene?

Eugene Off you go, Schoolmaster.

Furious, Bradley strides off after Charley. Mortimer looks after the departing figures.

Mortimer Lizzie Hexam? What have you done?

Eugene Nothing.

Mortimer I remember how that girl caught / your attention.

Eugene I pitied her. I've been visiting with her.

Mortimer Visiting?

Eugene Teaching her what I can.

Mortimer For God's sake, why?

Eugene She represents every lost soul in this city.
Every innocent life scarred by poverty and criminality.
I have a chance to help her.

Mortimer And is that all?

Eugene What else?

Mortimer You have a weakness.
I don't judge it, but . . .

Eugene This isn't like that!

Mortimer You're my best friend but I know you and I have to ask you.
Do you plan to capture and then desert this girl?

Eugene No!

Mortimer Do you plan to marry her?

Eugene Of course not.

Mortimer Can you assure me that your interest is *purely* educational?

Eugene I . . .

Mortimer Eugene.

Eugene Please stop.

Mortimer Do you plan to . . .

Eugene I don't plan anything! I've no design whatsoever!

Mortimer Then what are you doing?!

Eugene I've no idea.

Mortimer Give it up.

Eugene No.

Mortimer If not for yourself then for me,
for the sake of our partnership,
give it up.

Eugene I can't. I can't.

He turns quickly away, leaving Mortimer far behind.

Song: 'Eugene Alone'

Eugene

London's full of anger
I cannot express.
My mind, it only wanders
to the memory of her dress.

The night plays tricks upon me,
the streets become unknown.
I see her in the lamplight,
her dark eyes on the stone.

Can I find a way to stop this?
These thoughts I must repress.
Can I find a way to move on
from the memory of her dress?

I walk into the garden
put my hands into the earth,
and feel the pulse of London
take me back to her.

I felt her see into me
and now feel only shame.
She knows the sins I'm guilty of,
that I'm the one to blame.

And though I drink to forget
I still need to feel less,
to forget the way she saw me
and the memory of her dress.

As his song ends, Eugene moves off.

In her house, Jenny is working, Lizzie is by the fire. Bradley enters quickly.

Bradley Miss Hexam!

Jenny Oho!

Bradley I've come to talk with you.

Lizzie From Charley, sir?

Bradley I come of my own spontaneous act. Your brother has confided the whole matter to me.

Lizzie What matter, sir?

Bradley Charley is disappointed and I am disappointed. He had plans for you.
 Now we find that you have put your learning into the hands of this . . . lawyer?
 I resolved to come here and appeal to you directly.

Lizzie I'm sure, Mr Headstone, that your visit is well meant . . .

Bradley It is!

Lizzie But I've nothing to tell Charley except that I accepted the help *before*
   he made any plans for me. Jenny and I find our teacher very kind.

Bradley I wish I had been given the opportunity of coming here
   and devoting my poor abilities to your service.

Lizzie Thank you, sir.

Bradley I would have been *kind*.

Beat.

Lizzie I don't . . .

Bradley Say nothing! Only do well to remember the position you find yourself in.
   And the general opinion of you and your family.

Lizzie stares at him.

There's one thing more I have to say.
   There's a personal dimension to this matter.
   It might . . . I don't say it would, but it might . . .
   induce you to think differently.
   Not here, though. Not now.
   There must be another interview
   before the whole case can be submitted.

Lizzie What case, Mr Headstone?

Bradley You shall be informed in the other interview.
   I leave it all incomplete!
   There is a spell upon me, I think.

He stares for a second or two, then moves off quickly. A moment, then:

Jenny As I said . . . mighty *particular.*

Lizzie I'm sorry for him.

Jenny I don't think he could teach me anything
except how to drink blood and sleep in a coffin.
Not like Mr Wrayburn.

Lizzie Jenny.

Jenny You never want to talk about him.

Lizzie He's our teacher.

Jenny I wonder if he's rich?

Lizzie I don't think so, especially.

Jenny Handsome, though, isn't he?
Splendid and strong.

Lizzie Stop it.

Jenny Tell me how he makes you feel.

Beat.

Lizzie He makes me feel clear and muddy at the same time.

Jenny Do you love him?

Lizzie Of course not.

Jenny But if things were different.
If he were at our level . . .

Lizzie I don't know.

Jenny But you imagine it.

Lizzie We all dream, Jenny.

Jenny Speak it out.

A long beat, then Lizzie speaks.

Lizzie I know he has his failings,
but I think they've grown up

for the want of something to trust in.
I want to say to him,
'Only put me in that empty place inside you,
and see what a world of things
I will do and bear for you.'

A moment. Jenny shakes her head.

Jenny How can you think like that?

Lizzie Like what?

Jenny You're so much more
than the bearer of a man's burden.

Lizzie Don't get upset, dear.

Jenny I know you'll leave me in the end.
He'll ask
or another'll ask
and you'll go.

Lizzie No, Jenny.

Jenny Don't end the day with a lie, Liz.

She goes, leaving Lizzie alone.

The Boffin house. Bella comes into a room, laughing over her shoulder, Rokesmith is sitting there.

Bella Are you not enjoying the party?

Rokesmith I'm not really interested in society.

Bella I thought the same.
But I've just met the man who wants to get elected
and he's . . . fascinating.
He knows nothing of policy or government
or the people he's hoping to represent.
He's . . .

Rokesmith An idiot?

Bella Utterly.
I wonder if he'll win his election.

Rokesmith I think Mr Boffin's money will make sure of it.

Bella What are you reading?

Rokesmith It's nothing. An old notebook.

Bella (*reading the cover*) John Harmon?

Rokesmith It seems he kept a diary as a child.
Mr Boffin has kept some of his things.

Bella stares at the book.

I'm sorry.
I've reminded you of something painful.

Bella I don't need you to remind me, sir.
I think about it all the time.
The man drowned.
The man who drowned him.
His poor children.

Rokesmith You think of them all the time?

Bella Of course.
They didn't choose their parents.
None of us do.
What is it?

Rokesmith has stood and begun to pace.

Rokesmith I was just reflecting on the truth of what you said.
Our conversations mean a lot to me, Miss Wilfer.

Bella They do?

Stops pacing. Looks at her.

Rokesmith I wonder . . .

Boffin comes in, full of party energy.

Boffin Ho ho! Hiding in here? I don't blame you.
The conversation in there is thicker than Mrs Boffin's porridge.

Ever since I became rich,
it seems I'm only allowed to socialise with other rich people.
And they are dull beyond words.
Did you speak to anyone, Bella?

Bella I'm interested in the candidate.

Boffin In Veneering? Good Lord, you must be the first.

Bella He doesn't seem especially qualified.

Boffin No I suppose not.
But the seats must be filled.
All well, Secretary?

Rokesmith Yes, sir.

Boffin spots the notebook.

Boffin More Harmon artefacts?

Rokesmith Just a notebook.

Boffin The boy was always scribbling.
Always alone, poor lad.

Bella You loved him, Mr Boffin?

Boffin I felt responsible for him.
It was a hard fate, to be the son of my old master.
Mrs Boffin and I did what we could for the boy.
When we heard he was coming back, a grown man, well, we were excited.

Bella I'm sorry that you lost him.

Boffin We all lost him.
I'd swap the money in a heartbeat to have him back.

Noise from the room beyond.

Oho, Veneering is speaking.
Quick, Miss Wilfer, this could be a disaster.

He leaves at speed. Rokesmith sits very still.

Bella Are you coming, Mr Rokesmith?

Rokesmith Of course.

He follows.

Bradley and Charley near a graveyard, dawn.

Charley What we have got to do
is succeed this morning, Mr Headstone,
and then all the rest follows.

Bradley You're an optimist, Hexam.

Charley Everything is on our side.

Bradley Except your sister, perhaps?

Charley I know that she'll readily agree.
Here she comes.

Lizzie is on her way home from work.

Lizzie Why, Charley.
Where are you going?

Charley Nowhere. We came on purpose to meet you.

Lizzie Me?

Charley Come here into the churchyard, it's quiet.

Lizzie But it's not on my way.

Charley It's on my way, and my way is yours.
Mr Headstone has something to say to you.

Lizzie But . . .

Charley I'll go and take a little stroll and come back.
I know what he intends to say,
and I very highly approve of it.

Lizzie looks suddenly panicked.

Lizzie What does he want?

Charley You'll know soon.
Now, be a rational girl and a good sister.
Everything in our future depends on this.

Charley leaves. Lizzie and Bradley are alone.

Bradley I said when I saw you last, that there was something unexplained.
I have come this morning to explain it.
I hope you will not judge me.
It is most unfortunate for me
that I wish you to see me at my best,
and that I know you see me at my worst.
I can't help it. You are the ruin of me.

Lizzie Oh, sir.

Bradley Yes! you are the ruin, the ruin, the ruin of me.
I have no government of myself
when you are near me or in my thoughts.
And you are always in my thoughts.

Bradley's nose begins to bleed.

Lizzie Sir?

Bradley It's nothing!

He holds a handkerchief to his nose.

Lizzie I am grieved to have done you any harm.

Bradley There! Now I seem to have reproached you!
No man knows till the time comes
what depths are within him.
To me, you brought it; on me, you forced it;
and the bottom of this raging river
has been heaved up ever since.
You have done this to me.
Now you have to save me.

Lizzie Mr Headstone, I have heard enough.
Let us find my brother.

Bradley Not yet!
You could draw me to fire, to water,
to any exposure and disgrace.
But if you would return a favourable answer
to my offer of marriage,
you could draw me to every good with equal force.

Lizzie Mr Headstone –

Bradley Wait!
Before you answer me,
let's walk round this place once.
It will give you a minute's time to think,
and me a minute's time to get some fortitude together.

Lizzie nods. They walk in silence.

In Hampstead, Rokesmith sits in the dawn light. Bella enters.

Bella Mr Rokesmith?

Rokesmith You're awake.

Bella I find it hard to sleep at the moment.

Rokesmith I'm sorry to hear it.

Bella I'm actually glad of the chance to speak to you.

Rokesmith Are you?

Bella I know that I have sometimes been rude to you, distant and aloof.
I'm sorry. You must not think ill of me.

Rokesmith I only think well of you.

Bella Well, good.

Rokesmith I am drawn to you.
And I think that you are drawn, somehow, to me.

Bella Drawn?

Rokesmith You have unlocked something.

Bella Mr Rokesmith.

Rokesmith Listen to me!
I want there to be an understanding between us.
I want to be honest with you. I am –

Bella SIR! If you have any generosity, you will say no more.
This is not honourable of you!

Rokesmith Honourable?
I am trying to make an honest declaration
of an honest devotion to you.

Bella Did you say devotion?

Rokesmith Love!

Bella Whatever it is. I don't want it.
You know the history of my being here.

Rokesmith That does not define you!

Bella Of course it does!
It's enough that I've already been willed away by men.
Now you too dispose of me in your mind,
and speculate in me.
Am I forever to be made the property of strangers?

Rokesmith I'm no stranger.

Bella Am I not worth more than the doll in the doll's house?

Rokesmith You are.

Bella I know nothing of you and you do not know me.

Rokesmith Allow me . . .

Bella No more, sir! No more!

Silence.

Rokesmith I understand.
   Forgive my offence, it carries its punishment with it.

Bella I'm glad I have spoken.
   I beg you not to take advantage of your position in this house
   to make my position in it disagreeable.

Rokesmith For you to suggest that I would
   confirms that indeed
   you do not know me.

Rokesmith leaves. Bella sinks into a chair.

Bradley turns to Lizzie.

Bradley Well? Is it yes or no?

Lizzie I hope you may find a worthy wife and be very happy. But it is no.

Bradley Is no short time necessary for reflection;
   no weeks or days?

Lizzie None whatever.

Bradley You are quite decided?

Lizzie I am.

With a great roar, he grabs her by the arms.

Bradley YOU WILL RUIN ME!

Lizzie Mr Headstone, let me go. Help!

Bradley It is I who should call for help!

Lizzie Please, sir!

Bradley AH!

He releases her with a shove and staggers away. His nose is bleeding again.

You spurn me!
   Though you are kind enough to Eugene Wrayburn.

Lizzie He has been good to me, sir.

Bradley Of course! You're a social experiment to him.
My self-respect lies under his feet,
and he treads upon it.

Lizzie No, sir.

Charley runs back to them.

Charley I heard shouting.

Bradley I will walk home by myself, Hexam.

Charley Sir?

Bradley Let me be.

Bradley leaves, handkerchief clasped to his face. Charley looks at Lizzie.

Charley What have you done?

Lizzie He asked me – you know he asked me –
to be his wife.

Charley And?

Lizzie And I told him that I could not be.

Charley Do you know that he is worth fifty of you?

Lizzie It may be so, but I will never marry him.

Charley You have that choice?
This was a way out!
Now all my endeavours to let go of the past,
to raise myself in the world,
are to be beaten down by your low whims?

Lizzie Have I ever thought of myself before, Charley?
You call me selfish if you want to.
I won't marry him.

Charley paces for a moment.

Charley Let's talk this over like brother and sister.
I should have had a little chat with you
before Mr Headstone spoke for himself.
That was a mistake but it's soon set right.
I'll tell Mr Headstone your answer is not final,
and that it will all come round by-and-by.

Lizzie I won't allow you to say any such thing.

Charley You won't?

Lizzie shakes her head.

Very well. You shall not disgrace me.
I'm climbing up out of the mire
and you shall not pull me down.

Lizzie Charley.

Charley You're a false sister.
I've done with you.

Lizzie Don't say that.

Charley Forever. I've done with you.

Charley goes. Lizzie is alone in the graveyard.

On a deserted street in the West End, Eugene is walking.

Eugene After many sleepless nights
I resolve to visit Lizzie Hexam and tell her how I feel.
I want to be more than a teacher to her.
With my heart full, I walk.

Rokesmith is walking over Hampstead Heath.

Rokesmith With Bella Wilfer's words resounding in my head
I walk and walk.

Lizzie stands and starts to walk.

Lizzie Charley's words ring in my ears.
I leave the graveyard and I walk towards the river.

In Hampstead, Bella walks out into the garden.

Bella I walk into the garden
as the first light spills over the Hampstead rooftops.

Rokesmith As I walk across the heath,
my father's dust swirling around me,
I mutter all the way: 'John Harmon is dead.
Cover him, crush him, keep him down!'

Lizzie I can hear his voice,
'Done with you forever.'
And I know he's right.
I have to get out of London.

Eugene I have to see her.
I am happy.

Bella I don't understand why I pushed away
the thing that might make me happiest in the world.
What's wrong with me?

Rokesmith I come up Parliament Hill
as day finally breaks.

Eugene Over the city.

Rokesmith Over a cursed past.

Lizzie A haunted present.

Bella An unknown future.

The lights change.

Chapter Six

UPSTREAM

Song: 'The City and the Field'
Company

>London is not England –
>The grease, the steam, the blood.
>The calloused hands
>On the tanning floor
>The debtors' prison
>The workhouse door.
>
>See the painted Queen
>In her marble shroud,
>Moving through the thieves and whores
>And the weeping London crowd.
>
>England is not London –
>The moor, the stream, the wold.
>The cleaving plough, the alehouse
>The highwayman, the priest.
>The gamekeeper, the grocer
>The butcher and the beast.
>
>See the country beggar
>Hauling down the track.
>See his beggar father
>With England on his back.
>
>London is not England.
>England is not London.
>London is not England.
>England is not London.

But you cannot (cannot)
escape (Lizzie)
But you cannot (Lizzie)
escape (Hexam)
But you cannot (cannot)
escape (Lizzie)
yourself.

Miss Potterson steps into a country pub. Very different from the Fellowship Porters, the Waterman is quiet, rural. The Landlady, Nancy, is reading a novel behind the bar. Lizzie is wiping tables. She looks up with a start.

Lizzie Miss Potterson?

Potterson Hello, Lizzie.

Lizzie What are you doing here?

Potterson Don't you know?

Lizzie I'm sure I don't.

Potterson You don't know why I left the Porters and came upstream?
Why I've been two nights on the road?
That pub's my life, Lizzie,
and I've never left it so long.
Bob Gliddery is in charge now – God help us –
and here I am.

Lizzie I don't understand.

Potterson Your friend Jenny sent word you'd gone missing.
I told her I'd do what I could.

Lizzie How is she?

Potterson Sick with worry.

Lizzie Poor Jenny. How did you find me?

Potterson Publicans stick together.
The landlord at the Kingfisher in Maidenhead

said there was a new girl working in Winterbrook.
Said she had the smell of Limehouse about her.
I knew it was you.

Potterson waves at Nancy.

A'right, Nancy?

Nancy (*nodding*) Abbie.

Potterson turns back to Lizzie.

Lizzie What do you want?

Potterson Take you home, of course.
The city's a sewer but it's where we belong.

Lizzie I'm not coming home.

Potterson Plenty come to me for help. It's the landlord's curse.
Most I throw out like yesterday's oysters.
But you I want to help, Lizzie.
Don't ask me why.
But here I am.

Lizzie The river's different up here.
And there's air.
I can't come back, miss.

Potterson Your father's gone!
Come home, Lizzie.

Lizzie I can't.

Potterson We aren't responsible for what our men do.
My husband was a bastard.
He did terrible things across many terrible nights.
Those sins are not mine.

Lizzie I've never heard you talk of him.

Potterson Because he's gone!
And Gaffer's gone.

Lizzie But Charley isn't gone.
And for Charley's sake I've left.

Potterson What's it to do with Charley?

Lizzie I won't say any more.
I can't come back, not ever.

Potterson You have to live.
What are you afraid of?

Lizzie I'm grateful for you coming.
I truly am.

Potterson Always grateful but never bending.
Look at me.
You're the closest thing I have.
Come home.

Lizzie No.

Potterson For me.

Lizzie I can't.

Beat.

Potterson Lord knows I've tried to help you.
No more. I'm back to Limehouse.

She moves away.

Lizzie Will you tell Jenny that I'm safe?

Potterson For her sake I will.

Lizzie Only her.
Don't tell anyone else, no matter who comes asking.

Potterson These secrets'll rot you away from the inside.
I won't see you again.

Potterson leaves. Lizzie sits.

Nancy Need anything, Lizzie?

Lizzie Nothing.
I'll get back to work.

Lizzie stands.

In the study of the Boffin house, Rokesmith is packing a bag.

Boffin Mr Secretary!

Rokesmith Mr Boffin.

Boffin Are you ill, sir?

Rokesmith No. Not at all.

Boffin We missed you at breakfast yesterday.
And lunch and dinner.
I had no conversational companion!

Rokesmith I apologise.

Boffin Mrs Boffin cooked a pigeon for you.

Rokesmith Please extend to her my apologies.

Boffin And Miss Wilfer missed you.

Rokesmith That I doubt.

Boffin Don't be fooled by her sharp manners.
She's growing fond of us all.

Rokesmith I'm leaving, sir.

Boffin Beg pardon?

Rokesmith I offer you my resignation.

Beat.

Boffin Not accepted.

Rokesmith I'm afraid I must leave.

Boffin Somewhere to go? Something to do?

Rokesmith Neither.

Boffin Then why, man?
Gads, your an odd fish but I *like* you.
I like having you creeping about.
And I can't manage the dust without you.

Rokesmith I'm sorry. You'll need a new secretary.

Boffin thinks.

Boffin Ten pound a year more.

Rokesmith It's not the money.

Boffin Nothing better to do and not about the pay?
(*Suddenly beady.*) It's her, isn't it?

Rokesmith I offered her my esteem.
She assured me it was of no interest to her.
That's her prerogative.
But it means I cannot stay.

Boffin This is fluffy nonsense!

Rokesmith Please, Mr Boffin.
I hope I have done my job well.
You must allow me to leave.

Beat.

Boffin You are fixed?

Rokesmith Quite fixed.

Boffin Well I don't like it
And I shan't say I do!
Where are you going to go?

Rokesmith I don't know.

Boffin You are the strangest fellow.

Rokesmith picks up his bag.

Rokesmith Goodbye, Mr Boffin.

He leaves the house.
Boffin walks out of the room, shaking his head.

Boffin Oh dear dear dear.

Bella comes through the house towards him.

Oh dear dear dear.

Bella What is it, sir?

Boffin Come and sit, child.

He motions her to a chair.

Bella Is something wrong?

Boffin Why yes. My secretary has left.

Bella Left?

Boffin Resigned his employment and gone from the house.
Do you know why?

Beat.

Bella I think so.

Boffin He told me what had passed between you.
And I don't blame you, my dear.
But, think. Could you not grow to esteem him?
When Mrs Boffin met me
She thought me an utter vegetable.
A turnip in my looks and manners.
But see, she has grown to tolerate me.
(*Looks at Bella.*) Oh now, my dear, you are upset!

Bella has quite suddenly begun to cry.

Bella No, sir.

Boffin stands, awkward around the emotion.

Boffin I'll fetch Mrs Boffin.

Bella No, really!
Did Mr Rokesmith say where he would go?

Boffin I expect he'll vanish now,
as strangely as he came.

Bella I expect so.

Boffin I think you esteemed him more than you let him know, p'raps?

Bella I don't know.

Boffin Maybe you should have cast him a glance or two?

Bella Mr Boffin . . .

Boffin Encouraged him a little?

Bella Please, sir.

Boffin If you ever want my advice on such matters . . .

Bella Please, sir! Enough!

Bella runs outside the house.

***Song:* 'Holloway'**

Bella

> My world was
> Father, sister, mother,
> The Holloway Road,
> The chimneys and trees,
> And then, then you walked in
> And you saw me.
>
> The picture has changed.
> The air is not the same.
> The Holloway Road,
> The chimneys and trees,
> And then, then you walked in
> And you saw me.
>
> I confess I hated being poor.
> I confess that I loved being rich,
> But you didn't see the money
> Or you couldn't see the money –
> You saw me.

I ran from the pity
In your eyes upon me
When you spoke
Words like 'love' –
Then I knew that you saw me
And understood.

The picture has changed
The air is not the same.
I shut the door on your love
When you saw me and understood.

I confess I hated being poor.
I confess that I loved being rich,
But you didn't see the money,
Or you couldn't see the money –
You saw me.
You saw me.
You saw me.
You saw me.

Now the air is different
Now you're gone.
The streets of London
Are empty now.
The air is different
Now you're gone.
North London
Is empty now.

She moves off.

Eugene and Mortimer walk into the square.

Mortimer This hovel is the site of your little school?

Eugene Be serious. The girl is missing.

Mortimer She's an adult. She can go where she likes.

Eugene You don't know her. Or the world she lives in.

Mortimer And you do?

Eugene Something has happened.

Mortimer Eugene, I understand.

Eugene You do not.

Mortimer My life hasn't always been precedents and trials.
I've known infatuation.

Eugene Mortimer, please.

Mortimer But I say this to you as your friend.
If the girl's run away from you, it is futile to pursue her.
She has made a choice.

Eugene Nothing in her life has ever been a choice.
I need to find her.

Mortimer Look at you.
Your blood's pumping, your eyes are shining.
You love the hunt.
But what if it's you she's running from?

Eugene glares at him and knocks on the door.

Jenny Come in if you're good. But don't expect much.

They enter Jenny's room. She looks terrible.

Eugene Jenny. Are you sick?

Jenny How would I know, sir?

Eugene I've come . . .

Jenny I know why you've come.
The hero, returned to rescue the damsel in distress.

Eugene Have you heard from Lizzie?

Jenny Not me, though.
My suffering isn't pretty enough.

Eugene I'm sorry you are suffering.

Jenny *Are* you?

Eugene I need to know where she is.

Jenny It's like a fairytale from your books.
  Where does that leave the likes of me?

Eugene Jenny, please!

Jenny Just imagine.
  'I've come to save you, Jenny!'

Eugene TELL ME!

Mortimer Eugene.

  Beat.

Eugene I'm sorry. Sorry.

Jenny She's safe.

Eugene Tell me where.

Jenny I cannot, sir. I'm sworn.

Eugene Please.

Jenny It's impossible.
  You can shout all you want.
  You can strike, like men do.
  I am sworn.

Eugene I would never strike you.
  I am glad at least to know she is safe.

  Silence.

Mortimer We'll keep you no further, miss.
  (*To Eugene.*) We should go.

Eugene If you hear anything more.
  If she needs me . . .

Jenny I'll be sure to shout, Mr Wrayburn.

Eugene I hope you feel better.

Jenny Yes, that's worth hoping for.

Eugene and Mortimer leave. Outside in the square:

Eugene I'll find her somehow.

Mortimer You know the girl is safe. Let her be.
If you want to help someone
why not carry on teaching this poor thing?

Eugene You don't understand!

Suddenly Mr Cleaver emerges.

Mr Cleaver Gentlemen, good gentlemen.

Mortimer Leave us alone. We've nothing for you.

Mr Cleaver But I've something for you.
You want to know about the Limehouse girl.

Eugene Do you know something?

Mortimer Leave him, he's a wreck.

Mr Cleaver A visitor this morning, to my Jenny. A pub woman.
News of the girl.

Eugene grabs him. Mr Cleaver barely notices.

Eugene Tell me!

Mr Cleaver They think I can't hear.
Think I'm always sleeping.
I'm not *always* sleeping.

Eugene Tell me!

Mr Cleaver (*cunning*) What's it worth?

Eugene I've a pound note in my pocket.

Mortimer Eugene!

Mr Cleaver I'd rather two.

Eugene I have one and you'll take it.

Mr Cleaver Alright. Let's see it.

Eugene pulls a note from his pocket.

Eugene Where is she?

Mr Cleaver Upstream. Village called Winter . . . something. Working in a pub.

Mortimer You can't trust this.

Eugene looks at Mr Cleaver for a moment. Then hands him the pound note.

Eugene Here.

Mr Cleaver Much obliged.

He takes the money and shuffles off.

Mortimer He'll spend that entirely on gin.

Eugene I don't care.

Mortimer You're going after her?

Eugene I need to speak to her.

Mortimer Even though she has chosen to leave
and doesn't want to be found?
Who's trying to control the girl now?

Eugene looks at him.

This obsessive need to *save*.
If you pursue this,
you won't be able to return to the law.
Will you ruin your life for her sake?

Eugene Get back to your desk, Mortimer.
I'm going to find her.

He marches away. Mortimer watches him, concerned.

Rokesmith is walking.

Rokesmith John Harmon is dead
and John Rokesmith has given up on life.

So without name I walk back to the river.
Determined to find the river serpent
and see if one lie at least can be untold
and the Hexam family redeemed.
When I arrive at the creek
I find the hole deserted
and the snake gone.

Rokesmith stands by the river. Then a voice in the darkness.

Potterson Who's there?

Rokesmith Nobody.

Potterson Rogue Riderhood?

Rokesmith One who seeks him.

Miss Potterson emerges from the shadows.

Potterson You don't belong down here.
Why are you after him?

Rokesmith Do you know where he is?

Potterson If I did I'd strangle him.
And his lies with him.

Rokesmith Lies about the Harmon murder?

Potterson Maybe.
(*Curious.*) Who are you?

Rokesmith No one.
But we share a common cause.
I want to see Gaffer Hexam's name cleared of murder
and the shame lifted from his children.

Potterson Then good luck to you.
If you find him, come and tell me.
I'm at the Fellowship Porters in Limehouse.

Rokesmith I will.

Potterson And get in the warm, sir.
You look like a ghost.

Potterson leaves. Rokesmith looks at the river.

Eugene Wrayburn enters the Waterman. Nancy is reading her book.

Eugene I'm looking for a girl.

Nancy We're not that kind of pub.

Eugene A *particular* girl.
Lizzie Hexam.

Nancy Right.

Eugene Do you know her?

Nancy Seems to me
that's entirely my business.

Eugene She's been working here.

Nancy regards him for a moment.

Nancy Is she here now?

Eugene looks around.

Eugene I don't think so.

Nancy Then I can't help you.

Beat.

Eugene I need to see her. I need to know where she is.

Nancy And I said, I can't help.
Buy a drink or leave my pub.

Eugene leans forward, conspiratorially.

Eugene I'll pay.

Nancy This isn't London.
I'll do you the favour of pretending I never heard you say that.

But if you say it again
I've a cudgel beneath this bar
the exact size and shape of your head.

Eugene meets her eyes. She's serious.

Eugene I'm renting a room in the village.
I'll come back tomorrow.

Nancy I hope not.

With a final, frustrated look around, Eugene leaves the pub. Outside, he turns his collar up against the night.

Eugene (*under his breath*) Where the hell are you?

He turns and bumps into a hooded stranger who was hovering in the night.

Watch out!

Stranger Pardons, guv'nor.

Eugene strides off. The stranger lowers his hood.

Riderhood When that man with no name came visiting
I thought I'd best be away for a while.
I always liked coming upstream:
the cowshit and the brambles.
I was pissing against a boathouse
when I saw this one
trudging up the riverbank.
One of them lawyers.
Looking for something. Looking for me?
I'll find out.

Rogue Riderhood turns to follow Eugene. Suddenly another voice from the shadows.

Voice You.

Riderhood Speaking to me?

Voice I am.

Riderhood No one speaks to me.

Voice Do you know that man?

Riderhood What man?

Voice The one you've been following.

Riderhood Who's asking, in the dark?

Voice One who you would do well to respect.

Riderhood Ha. Earn it.
Why you asking about him?

Bradley Headstone steps forward into the lamplight.

Bradley I've watched you follow him for miles.
I know because I've followed him myself.
All the way from London.
Do you know him?
Answer me, you country clod.

Riderhood I'm no country nothing!
I know the lawyer.
I wanna know if he's here for me.
And now I wanna know you, an' all.

Bradley My identity's of no concern to you.
Let us say I'm one
with an interest in that man and his future.
If I found a fellow willing to help me secure that future . . .

Riderhood Secure?

Bradley lowers his voice.

Bradley I want him gone.
I'd be grateful.

Riderhood You're talking about dark work, sir.
With your nice coat and your clean nails.
I'm not sure you're cut out for it.

Bradley But you are.

Riderhood You think you know me?
I've done things would make you
never close your eyes again if I told you.
But I won't be commissioned into darkness no more.
Not for all your gold.
Never mind the lawyer.
Get yourself gone.

Bradley I'm a man of substance!
I won't be scared away.

Riderhood GET GONE!
Or I'll feed you to the country pigs.

Riderhood lunges for Bradley, who turns and runs away into the darkness.
   Lizzie, carrying a bag, walks out of the Waterman. Nancy steps in front of her.

Nancy That you off then?

Lizzie Nancy.

Nancy Were you going to say goodbye?

Lizzie There was a man here. Asking about me.

Nancy He didn't look like much.
I mentioned my cudgel and he nearly fell over.
Nothing to be afraid of.

Lizzie I have to keep moving.

Nancy Can I do anything?

Lizzie (*shaking her head*) Old ghosts, that's all.
Thanks for the work and board.

Nancy Find your place, Lizzie.
No one can run forever.

Lizzie looks at her, pulls the bag on her shoulder and steps out into the night.

Song: 'Upstream'

Lizzie

> There's a time late at night
> When the river rises.
> There's a time late at night
> When it rises to meet the land.
> And there's nothing, nothing to do
> But think on my sins.
> And there's nothing, nothing to do –
> Sins lifted by the tide, the tide.
>
> Upstream beyond the city
> The river is running the same.
> I hear the water whisper
> A curse upon my name.
>
> And the ghosts are singing, the ghosts,
> The ghosts are singing, the ghosts –
> A long, sad song of shame.

Bradley and Eugene join her and they all sing.

Lizzie, Bradley *and* **Eugene**

> There's a time before the dawn
> When the river, the river falls.
> There's a time before the dawn
> When it falls back from the bank.
> And there's nothing, nothing to do
> But step into the light.
> And there's nothing, nothing to do –
> I'm alone again, again and
>
> Upstream beyond the city
> The river is running the same.
> I hear the water whisper
> A curse upon my name.
>
> And the ghosts are singing, the ghosts,
> The ghosts are singing, the ghosts,
> The ghosts are singing, the ghosts.

Lizzie

I turn back, and set to work again.

By the end of the song, the sun has risen around Lizzie. Carrying her bag, she walks down the river. Bradley is watching her.

Bradley (*to himself*) I'll not be dragged under the waves.
Time to stand up.
(*Calling out.*) Miss Hexam.

Just as he does so, Eugene appears on the towpath.

Eugene Lizzie!

Lizzie Mr Wrayburn?

Bradley pulls back into the shadows.

Eugene Please wait.
Just allow me to speak to you.
Please.
I'm so happy to see you.

He takes a step towards Lizzie, and as he does so . . .
Bradley rushes forward with a cry, picking up a rock as he moves. He smashes it down upon Eugene's head.

Lizzie (*scream*) No!

The hooded Bradley hits Eugene twice more with the rock. Blood begins to pour.

Bradley (*in Lizzie's direction*) STAY BACK!

As Lizzie watches, stricken, Bradley pushes the body into the river. Eugene starts to drown.
Bradley runs away. Lizzie rushes to the bank.

Lizzie Help! Someone help me!

She looks around desperately. The riverbank is deserted. Throwing down her bag, taking off her shoes, Lizzie jumps into the water.

Chapter Seven

THE THING CALLED HOME

In the Wilfer house, Mary is making breakfast. Reg is dashing around, getting ready to leave for work.

Mary (*calling upstairs*) Lavinia. Bacon.

Reg My dear, did you see my hat?

Mary It's on the hook.

Reg Is it?

Mary (*weary*) Yes.

Reg Oh, thank you.

He finds the hat, kisses the top of her head, walks to the door.

Hello! Where's the doorplate?

Mary Now he notices!

Reg It's gone.

Mary Two days ago.

Reg But *where's* it gone?

Mary The man came with a pair of pincers
and took it off and took it away.
He said that as he had not been paid
and as he had another order for a Girls' School doorplate,
he was having it back.

Reg Perhaps it's for the best, my dear.

Mary The best!

Reg Perhaps it's time to let go
of the dream of a School for Girls . . .

Mary Oh indeed?
Let all the dreams go!
I wonder you can carry on, RW.

Reg What do you mean?

Mary You come and go, work and sleep.
Hats and doorplates!
And all the while, your daughter's lost.

Reg Oh my dear, not lost.

Mary I shan't cry over the bacon again.
But, yes, I say lost.
You're the master here, not I,
But I don't know how you do it.
(*Shouting again.*) LAVINIA! BACON!

Reg We saw Bella ten days ago.
We'll see her again soon.

Mary Ten days?
To a mother, it may as well be ten years.
You don't feel it.

Reg I do. I miss Bella very much.
But she is grown-up and . . .

Mary LAVINIA!

Lavinia appears, mid-shout.

Lavinia I'm here.

Mary Sit and eat!
Grown-up indeed.

Lavinia Who's grown-up? Me?

Mary You're still a girl.

Reg Mary.

Mary A girl! You don't know head from heels.

Lavinia I do know them and if you say that,
you watch and I'll be gone out of the door as well.

Mary Oh! You hear, RW! You hear! They'll both go!

Reg Lavinia won't go anywhere.

Lavinia Won't I?!

Reg No. You're a good girl.

Lavinia Am I?!

The door has opened. Bella stands there. She holds a loaf of bread.

Bella Hello. I brought this.

Looking from her daughter to the bread and back again, Mary immediately bursts into tears.

Mary Oh Bella!

Bella Mother? It's just bread.

Mary I miss you.

Bella comforts Mary. Reg looks at Bella.

Reg Are you alright, my dear? This is a surprise.

Bella I'm fine.

Lavinia Have you come home?

Bella No. I just . . .
(*To Mary.*) I missed you too.

Mary (*new sob*) Oh!

Reg There's bacon in the pan, Bella.
So now we've a loaf, sandwiches!

Bella Lovely.

Beat.

Is Mr . . .

Reg What, dear?

Bella Mr Rokesmith.

Mary (*fierce*) Don't speak his name!

Bella Why?

Mary Gone in the night.
With not a word.

Lavinia We knew he was a wrong'un!

Reg My dears, be fair.
He left his outstanding rent
and a note, saying he'd been called away.

Lavinia On the run!

Reg watches Bella, curious.

Reg Do you know anything about his departure, Bella?

Bella No.
He left Mr Boffin's employ quite suddenly as well.

Reg I expect a young man like that
has all manner of romantic intrigues going on.

Lavinia He's like a man in my book, a mysterious killer . . .

Mary Bella?

Bella has started crying.

Bella I'm sorry. I don't know what's wrong with me.

Reg Oh come here, child.

Lavinia What is it?

Bella I made a mistake.
He's gone.
And I . . .
I don't belong there. Don't belong here.

I can't come home, even if I wanted to.
And he's gone.

Reg Now then, now then.
There's nothing we can't fix together.

Suddenly, noisily, Boffin enters.

Boffin Hello hello!

Mary Mr Boffin?

Boffin Mrs Wilfer! And Mr . . . and . . .
(*Spotting Bella.*) Oh dear oh dear. Still crying?

Mary Has she been upset?

Boffin I'm afraid that young love has its twists.
But look here, Bella.
Never let it be said that Noddy Boffin
allowed heartache to go untreated.
A clue!

He is brandishing a piece of scrap paper.

Bella What's that?

Boffin My secretary left it behind.
Now I don't say it's where he's gone,
but I do say it's a clue. Only one we have.
And it should be followed.

He hands it to Bella.

Bella It's an address on the river. Deptford Creek.

Reg takes the paper and looks at it.

Reg Wretched part of the city.

Lavinia He *is* a murderer.

Reg Hush, Lavinia.
(*Looks at Bella.*) If you need to speak to him
we'd better go and see if we can find him?

Bella looks at her father.

Bella You'll come with me?

Reg I have to go to work this morning,
but tonight we shall go downriver together.

Boffin I'll lend you the carriage!

Reg Settled then.
Now eat your bacon and dry your tears.
(*Putting his hat on.*) Mary, Lavinia, I love you all.

He moves to the door.

Boffin I'll lift you into the city, sir!

Reg Thank you, Mr Boffin, but I like the walk.
London's best on foot.

Boffin Very well. Good day good day to all.
And courage, Miss Wilfer!
Love shall prevail.

Both Boffin and Reg leave. Mary pours tea for Bella, who begins to cut the bread.
   Lavinia watches her sister for a while.

Lavinia (*grudging*) It is *quite* nice to have you back.

Bella Thank you, Lavvy. How's your book?

Lavinia You'll never guess, it was the old woman that did it!

Bella *I knew it!*

They laugh together. Mary sobs noisily.

Mary Oh!

Bella What now?

Mary You two!

She embraces them both. The lights change.

Bradley enters Mortimer's rooms.

Mortimer Can I help you?

Bradley Ah – yes. Yes, sir.

Mortimer Are you in need of legal advice?

Bradley Legal! No.

Mortimer Then I'm afraid you may have wasted your journey.
Legal advice is all I offer.

Bradley You're Mortimer Lightwood?

Mortimer I am.

Bradley The lawyer responsible for the Harmon case?

Mortimer Correct.

Bradley I'm a friend of Charles Hexam. I'm his schoolmaster.

Mortimer Then I am pleased to meet you, sir.
Can I offer you a drink?

Bradley Tell me where she is.

Mortimer I'm sorry?

Bradley Lizzie Hexam.

Beat.

Mortimer You're looking for Lizzie?

Bradley I . . . we, Charley and I . . .
we need to know where she is.
He needs to know if she is safe.

Mortimer Well, it so happens I can help you.
I spoke with Miss Hexam not two hours ago.

Bradley S-spoke to her?

Mortimer Saw her, spoke with her.
She is quite safe, you can tell your pupil.

Bradley She's in London?

Mortimer And with an astonishing tale to tell.
She has had an appalling few days.
She was upstream, staying in the country
when she witnessed an attempted murder.

Bradley Attempted?

Mortimer Had it not been for her,
Eugene Wrayburn would have drowned.
We owe her my friend's life.

Bradley looks like he might faint.

Bradley Where is she now?

Mortimer She's back in Limehouse
Staying at an inn owned by a friend of hers.
Charley knows it, I'm sure.

Bradley suddenly stands.

Bradley I'll tell him.

Mortimer Please send him my best, Mr . . .

Bradley It doesn't matter.

Mortimer No? Very well.
When I next see Miss Hexam, I'll . . .

But Bradley has gone. Confused, Mortimer returns to his books.
  In the street outside, Charley is waiting for Bradley.

Charley Mr Headstone?

Bradley Hexam.

Charley Are you ill?

Bradley Just . . . give me a moment.

Charley What happened, sir?

Bradley I'll be alright.

Charley I wish you'd let me come up, sir.
Mr Lightwood may have remembered me.

Bradley He did remember you.

Charley Did he know about Lizzie?

Bradley She is back in Limehouse.

Charley What?! Whereabouts?

Bradley Some public house.

Charley The Porters? What's she doing there?

Bradley looks up with fury.

Bradley She's with him! With Wrayburn.

Charley (*thinking*) She must be having more lessons . . . .

Bradley Lessons? Your sister is deep in sin, Hexam.
She is lost.

Charley Don't speak like that.
She isn't lost! Not to him.

Bradley You must face the truth of who and what she is.

Charley Please, sir. Come with me to Limehouse.
We'll find out what hold he has on her.
Please!

They move quickly away, Bradley still swaying uneasily.

In the Fellowship Porters, a bed has been set up. Eugene lies there, still bruised and bloodied from the assault. Lizzie is changing the dressing on his head wound.

Lizzie How's your eye?

Eugene Still sore.

Lizzie Can you hear anything on this side?

Eugene Mercifully not.
I think Bob Gliddery was singing again this morning . . .

Lizzie We'll soon get you home.

Eugene For what? I can't work now.

Lizzie Mr Lightwood said he knew of a nurse
who could look after you.

Eugene I don't need another nurse.

Beat. She goes on changing his bandages.

Do you remember our lesson on Soteria and Eurypylos?

Lizzie I remember everything.

Eugene Go on then.

Lizzie Eurypylos was an ancient king.
He set eyes upon the idol of Dionysus
and it sent him mad.
Nothing could help him.
Till he visited the sanctuary of Soteria.

Eugene Goddess of safety and salvation.

Lizzie He looked at her,
a young woman, crowned with laurels,
and he was cured.
He was saved.

Eugene When I opened my eyes on that riverbank
coughing up brown Thames water . . .
All I could see was you.
You're *my* Soteria, Lizzie.
You saved me.

Beat.

You know how I feel about you.

Lizzie Mr Wrayburn, please don't.

Eugene Eugene.
I love you.
Beyond reason and time, I love you.
BELIEVE ME.

Lizzie I do believe you.

Eugene And you love me.
   In spite of what you tell yourself.
   You threw yourself into that river without a thought.
   You love me.

Lizzie It doesn't matter.

Eugene It matters above everything!

Lizzie No!
   You can't marry the daughter of a dockside murderer.
   And I . . .

Eugene What?

Lizzie I'm not a goddess!
   I saved you from the river.
   That doesn't make me your salvation.

   Beat.

For a long time
   I have dreamt about loving you.
   Holding you up, the way I held up Father.
   It's just a dream.

Eugene But I . . .

   Lizzie Don't say anything else.
   You have to go to a proper nurse.
   And I have to leave this place.
   Tonight.

Eugene Back to Winterbrook?

Lizzie Somewhere.
   I mustn't do anything to harm Charley's chances.

Eugene For Christ's sake, listen to me.
   Enough martyr.
   Enough sacrifice to Father, brother.

What do you want?
What do YOU want?

Beat.

Lizzie In my secret heart, I think I want things.
Sometimes I can't even put words to them.
Maybe I want to travel.
Maybe I want to go to school myself.
Maybe I want to live with Jenny.
Maybe I want to marry you.
I don't even know how to begin
to choose for myself.

Potterson comes in.

Potterson There's someone here to see you.

She reveals Jenny.

Lizzie Jenny!

She embraces Jenny.

I'm so happy to see you.

Jenny You say that.
But you *look* sad.
How's your poor heart, my dear?

Lizzie I'm sorry I had to go away, Jenny.
I have missed you.

Jenny (*simple*) I have missed you like a part of my own body.
Like a part of my own heart had gone upstream.
But here you are safe.
Is he here? The romantic lead?

Lizzie Sssh! He's had a terrible ordeal.

Jenny I heard you saved him.
He thought he was the dashing hero,
turns out it was you.
Ooh, I hooted when I heard.

Lizzie Jenny . . .

Jenny Well you're both safe.
Now when are you coming home?

Lizzie Home?

Jenny I've kept your bed made up in your corner.
The dolls and I are ready to receive you.
You are coming home?

Suddenly, a banging on the door.

Bradley OPEN THIS DOOR.

Bradley and Charley are outside the pub. Bradley hammers on the door.

Potterson What the hell?

Bradley We've come for Lizzie Hexam.
We know she's here.

Lizzie looks at Potterson in desperation.

Lizzie Help me.

Potterson Both of you, down the back, quickly.

Lizzie nods and, helping Jenny, moves off. Once they are gone:

Who are you? What do you think you're doing?

Charley Miss Potterson, it's Charley.
We need to speak to Lizzie.

Potterson Charley Hexam?
Get a grip on yourself.
I won't have this.

Bradley He's in there!
I know he's in there with her.

He bangs again.

Charley Mr Headstone, please.

Potterson YOU STEP AWAY FROM MY DOOR RIGHT NOW.
There's an Inspector
who's a particular friend of this house.
If there is one more word out there
He'll bring his mastiff
And have your balls.
Men have underestimated me before.
Go on, TRY ME.

Beat. Breathing deeply, Bradley moves away from the door. He stands in the street, looking completely lost. His nose starts bleeding.
 Charley stares at him.

Charley Mr Headstone?
Sir, there's blood.

Then a voice behind them:

Riderhood Blood all over this one.

Bradley slowly turns. Stares at Riderhood.

Bradley I've nothing to say to you.

Riderhood You had words enough for me upstream,
didn't you, Mr Learned Teacher?
Had words when you offered me
money to kill the lawyer?

Beat.

Charley What's he talking about?

Riderhood And you had more than words
the next morning.

Bradley What did you say?

Riderhood I saw ya.
You picked up a rock and you went for him.
I know murder, Mr Learned Teacher.

Lived with it all my life.
I know when a man strikes to kill.
And you struck.

Bradley Get away from me.

Charley Mr Headstone.

Riderhood I'm sorry, Charley boy.
I carried you as a baby.
Gaffer was my partner.
I shouldn't ever have 'cused him.
This one, I 'cuse him gladly.

Charley stares at Bradley, who has blood on his face.

Charley You didn't.

Bradley It was all for the best.

Charley You struck him?

Bradley He's got a hold on her!
If I hadn't stopped him
he'd have taken her away from us.

He lurches towards him desperately.

Charley . . .

Charley jerks away.

Charley Don't touch me!
I thought you were something else.
A chance of something else.
But you're here, in the filth
with the likes of *him*.
I don't know you.

*And shaking his head, Charley leaves.
Bradley turns on Riderhood.*

Bradley You flotsam. You wash-up.
I'll cut your throat.

He starts towards Riderhood, who stops him with his voice, soft and dangerous.

Riderhood I've already warned you, Mr Learned Teacher.
If you take another step towards me
it's a step into the depths.
I've been down there before.
I've held men under the water,
held 'em till their bodies stopped twitching.
Take another step and you'll join 'em down there.
I've a life that's not much to lose.
What about you?

Bradley stares at him for a long time, then launches himself at Riderhood.
  Rokesmith appears.

Rokesmith I finally spot him across the cobbles
the river serpent
who alone can lift the curse from the Hexam name.
He's locked in a vicious embrace with another:
two men, wrestling in the shadows.
I watch as they struggle, watch as they fall,
watch as the water engulfs them.
I stare at the broiling river
to see which one will surface.
But neither does.
The Thames swallows them up
and with them the last living record
of the fate of John Harmon.
I can't help the Hexams.
I'll never see Bella again.
I cannot move forward.
I am resolved.
I step towards the water.

Song: 'Deptford Creek'

Rokesmith

> The Thames is so dark,
> There are no reflections.
> The river flows
> Down past the Creek.
> The sky and the water
> Blacker than oil.
>
> The lanterns go out,
> Swallow the night.
> The London tide turns heavy.
> The moon's the only light.
>
> Deptford is all –
> Deptford around me.
> Midnight bells
> Summon the drunks.
> Night owls calling.
> Smuggler's tales.
>
> The lanterns go out,
> Swallow the night.
> The London tide turns heavy.
> The moon's the only light
>
> As the lanterns go out,
> Swallow the night.
> The London tide turns heavy.
> The moon's the only light.
>
> Here is the place,
> The place where I died.
> Why?
> Why?
> Why?
> Without love there is no answer.
> Without love there is no answer.
> Without love there is no answer.

Without love there is no answer.
Without love there is no answer.
Without love there is no answer.

Bella Mr Rokesmith?

Rokesmith turns, to find Bella staring at him.

Rokesmith Is this coincidence?

Bella No.
I came looking for you.

Rokesmith At our last meeting
your feelings regarding my presence
in, or approximate to, your life,
were plainly expressed.

Bella I misspoke, sir.

Rokesmith I'm sorry?

Bella When Mr Boffin told me that you had left
I found . . .

Rokesmith What?

Bella I found that I was unhappy.

Rokesmith Unhappy.

Bella There *is* something between us, Mr Rokesmith.
I do not pretend to understand it.
But I feel it.
When you told me that you also felt it
I was afraid.
I was not kind and I did not treat you as you deserved.
I have . . .

Rokesmith Miss Wilfer.

Bella Please let me finish.
I think I am in –

Rokesmith MISS WILFER.

Bella falls silent.

I am not who you think I am.

Beat.

Bella I know almost nothing about you.
That does not stop me loving you.

Rokesmith Loving me . . .

Bella With my whole soul.

Beat.

Rokesmith Our first meeting was not an accident.
I knew you before you knew me.
My name is John Harmon.

Bella doesn't move.

Bella Say that again.

Rokesmith I am John Harmon.

Bella John Harmon died.

Rokesmith No.
A stranger died and was given my name.
I saw a chance to escape and I took it.

Bella Escape?

Rokesmith Escape the future my father had decreed.
His money, his choice of wife.
I wanted to run.
The stranger died and I saw my chance.

Bella shakes her head in incredulity.

Bella You're lying.

Rokesmith It is the purest truth.

Bella breathes, tries to steady herself.

Bella Then why did you not leave?
If you wanted to escape . . .

Why return to torment me?
This is cruelty.

Rokesmith No.
I never wanted to hurt you.
For two weeks I thought I could run.
But I couldn't forget the idea
of the woman my father had named.
Who'd been rendered a widow
because of my choices.
I had to see you, to know you.
And when I did . . .

Bella What?

Rokesmith I loved you.
From the first moment.
My father never did a thing in his life
for anyone but himself.
I don't know why he willed us together
but I know that when I look at you
I feel complete.

He steps towards her.

Bella . . .

Bella starts away.

Bella Don't.
This is too much.
When I came looking for you, tonight . . .

Rokesmith What?

Bella I thought there could be an understanding.

Rokesmith There still could.

Bella No.
I don't have the words for this.
I have to go.

She runs. He shouts after her.

Rokesmith Bella!

Reg steps out of the shadows, in front of his daughter.

Reg Stop, Bella. Stop.

He holds her.

Bella Let me go.

Reg For a moment, stop.
And look at me, my dear.
(*A sudden purposeful clarity.*) This world is strange, stranger than we know.
And it is hard.
There are so many things we can't choose.
Here is something you can.
Choose to love.
At least do yourself the good service
of thinking about it.
Don't run.

Bella He . . . he is John Harmon!

Reg Aye. So he is.
So he is.

Bella stares at her father.
  After a long time she turns and looks back at Rokesmith, from now on called John Harmon.

Bella What about the money?
If you are . . . coming back to life . . .
What about Mr Boffin?

Harmon He can have the money.
He'll do better with it than I will.

Bella He won't take it.

Harmon Then I'll give it away.
My father's fortune was nothing but the filth of the city

swept and heaped and turned to money.
What matters is you,
I can only return to the world
if I know that you're with me.

A long moment. Reg holds his breath. Harmon looks at Bella. Eventually . . .

Bella I'm with you.

Reg (*a quiet sigh*) There now.

Bella I'm with you.

Bella moves towards Harmon and slowly touches his cheek, seeing him as if for the first time.

You're cold.

Harmon Not so cold.

The lights change.

Chapter Eight

THE WHOLE CASE

Early hours of the morning in Limehouse. Charley leads Mortimer towards the Fellowship Porters.

Charley They were outside here, sir.
If they'll let us in
Someone might know where they've gone.

Mortimer You did the right thing, Charley.
It's not easy when a friend falls.
But it's the right thing.

Charley He was my schoolmaster. Not my friend.

Mortimer I understand.

Charley And we'll take 'em both, sir?
Riderhood told me he should never have named my father.

Mortimer He's been lying from the start.
The Inspector can arrest them both.
Hello! This is Mortimer Lightwood.
Miss Potterson?

Potterson opens the door.

Potterson Mr Lightwood?
Come in, sir.
Charley.

They move inside. There they find the Inspector, nursing a sherry.
  Lizzie and Jenny are sitting to one side. Eugene, his head bandaged, sits next to them.

Jenny Here's trouble.

Lizzie jumps to her feet as they enter.

Lizzie Charley!

Charley (*nodding*) Hello, Liz.

Mortimer walks across the room, the lawyer taking command.

Mortimer Inspector, I'm glad to find you.
(*He indicates Eugene.*) I know who attacked my friend here.
This boy had the confession from the man's own lips not two hours ago.

Inspector That right, Charley?

Charley Yes, sir.

Eugene slowly raises his bandaged head.

Eugene You know who attacked me?

Charley It was Mr Headstone. My schoolmaster.

He turns to Lizzie.

I didn't know, Liz.
I thought . . . he was better.
I didn't know.

Lizzie It's not your fault.

Charley He was here before.
You'll find him if you move fast.
Maybe he's gone back to the school . . .

Jenny No, he ain't.

Charley What do you mean?

The Inspector indicates two bodies, covered in sheets, that lie to one side.

Inspector Constable and I just hauled 'em out.

Charley stares for a long time.

Charley Dead?

Inspector I'm sorry, lad.

Charley shakes his head. He moves across the room towards his sister.

Charley Liz . . .

He tails off.

Lizzie What is it?

Charley I don't know how.

Lizzie How what?

Charley I need to ask you to forgive me
And I don't know how.
I thought I did all for the best.
But I'd have married you off to him
to secure my own future.
(*Staring at the floor.*) I'm sorry.

She takes his face in her hands.

Lizzie You listen to me.
I am yours and you are mine.
Cradle to grave.
I know you.
I forgive you.
I'm so proud of you.

They embrace. Jenny nudges Potterson.

Jenny Think we'll ever be done with it?

Potterson With what?

Jenny The endless job of forgiving men.

The door opens and Harmon and Bella enter the room. With them is Boffin.

Harmon Excuse me.

Potterson Can I help you?

Harmon I think some of you know me.
Inspector.

Inspector Yes?

Harmon We met the night John Harmon was murdered.
I came to identify the body.

Charley I remember. Turned you green.

Harmon You're Charley Hexam.
Forgive me, this is . . .
This is Bella Wilfer.

Mortimer Wilfer?

Bella Yes, sir.
I was John Harmon's widow.
(*Glancing at Harmon.*) Not any more.

Boffin Astonished faces!
Quite right.
I fainted clean away.
Mrs Boffin had to fetch the smelling salts . . .

Harmon We have some answers to your questions.
I gave my name that night as Rokesmith.
In fact, it is John Harmon.
The man who was murdered was a thief.
He stole clothes and papers from me
and I watched him die.
Beaten and thrown into the river for a few coins.

Lizzie glances at Charley.

Lizzie By our father?

Harmon No, miss. By the serpent known as Riderhood.
Gaffer Hexam killed no one that night.
Nor any night, as far as I know.

Beat. Lizzie sinks into a chair. Mortimer shakes his head in disbelief.

Mortimer *You* are John Harmon?

Harmon There are some things I'll explain.
Some things that defy explanation.

Bella But we needed to tell you that
your father was innocent.

Charley Inspector?

Inspector I'll take a statement from Mr Harmon here.
If what he says is true,
Gaffer's memory is clear.

Harmon moves towards Charley.

Harmon I know a little of the shadow
that this accusation has cast upon you.
Consider it lifted.

*Charley looks at Lizzie. Everyone else does the same.
Eugene pulls himself up in his chair to look at her.*

Eugene Lizzie? You're free.

*They stare at each other for a long time. Eventually,
Potterson comes around from behind the bar.*

Potterson The sun's coming up.
Those of you who are going to talk more
do it at the police station.
Those who are sleeping here,
go to bed.

*Everyone begins to move. Lizzie, shaky, walks towards
Bella.*

Lizzie Miss?

Bella looks at her.

Thank you.

Bella You're welcome.

Lizzie I don't really understand.

Bella You don't have to.
Not everything makes sense.
It's London.

Harmon has been with the Inspector.

Harmon Bella? The Inspector needs us.

Boffin We'll go together.

Mortimer I'm coming too. And you, Charley.

Charley Me?

Mortimer Perhaps we could talk? I'm in need of a junior clerk.

Charley Maybe, sir. I'll think about it.

Mortimer Please do that.

Charley looks back at his sister.

Lizzie I'll see you in the morning.

Charley nods and he leaves, along with Mortimer, the Inspector, Bella, Boffin and Harmon.

Jenny.

Jenny I know you're not coming back, Liz.
You don't have to say it.

Jenny moves towards the door.

Potterson You don't have to go back there.

Jenny Says who?

Potterson Stay here. If you want.
You can have Bob Gliddery's bed.

Jenny Live in a pub?
Think what my father'd say.
Show me, then.

Jenny and Potterson leave.
Lizzie and Eugene are alone. A long moment.

Lizzie Hello. I . . .

Eugene Wait.
There are some things I want to say.
I want to ask you to come over here.
I want to tell you that the stain on your family is lifted
and that you are free.
I want to kiss you
and tell you that we can be married.

Lizzie can't reply.

Eugene I want to.
But I won't.

She stares at him.

I'm no ancient hero, Lizzie.
I'm a foolish man with a very sore head.
And you're right.
You're not my salvation.

Lizzie No.

Eugene You are whatever you want to be.
I'll be forever grateful for what you've done for me,
but I'm not your father.
I don't own your future.

Lizzie You. Jenny. Charley.
I don't know what my future is.

Eugene Then go and find it.
If any of us are in it,
that'll be our very good fortune.
It's for you to choose.
You're free.

Beat.

Lizzie I'm afraid.

Eugene I know.

Lizzie But that's as it should be.

Outside, on the river, the sun begins to rise.

The sun's rising. Time to wake up.
London.

Lizzie steps away from him, out into the morning.

Song: 'Homecoming'

Company

>The grey light of dawn
>on flagstones and parks.
>The grey light of dawn
>on bridges and the docks.
>
>Clearing to daylight.
>Creeping back to life.
>
>The flowing, filthy river
>the timber and the mud.
>The tide always returning
>the tenderness of dawn.
>
>London, remembered.
>London, forgiven.
>
>Ooooooooo
>Ooooooooo
>Oooo Oooo
>
>For all our pasts remembered
>as tide baptises stone,
>and all our pasts forgiven,
>London is our home.
>
>London, remembered.
>London, our future.

The End.